HE HAD ME AT 'OLÉ'

HE HAD ME AT 'OLÉ'

A rollicking tale
of socially awkward
passion, patatas
& polka dots

Stacey M. Erbacher

© 2023 Stacey M. Erbacher

2nd edition.

The moral rights of the author have been asserted.

All rights reserved. No part of this book may be reproduced by any mechanical, photographic, electronic process, audio recording, nor can it be stored in a retrieval system, copied or transmitted in any form or by any means for public or private use – other than for "fair use" as brief quotations embodied in articles and reviews – without the prior written permission of the author, nor be otherwise circulated in any form of binding or cover other than that in which it is published and without a similar condition being imposed on the subsequent purchaser.

The author has made every effort to ensure the accuracy of the information within this book was correct at the time of publication. The author does not assume and hereby disclaims any liability to any party for any loss, damage or disruption caused by errors or omissions, whether such errors or omissions result from accident, negligence, or any other cause. Some names and descriptions have been changed for privacy.

A catalogue record for this book is available from the National Library of Australia.

ISBN 978-0-6453440-1-1 (paperback)
ISBN 978-0-6453440-0-4 (ebook)

Cover design & interior artwork by Spider House
Typesetting by Kirby Jones

www.wanderswithwit.com

For
Vicente, Ethel & Jim

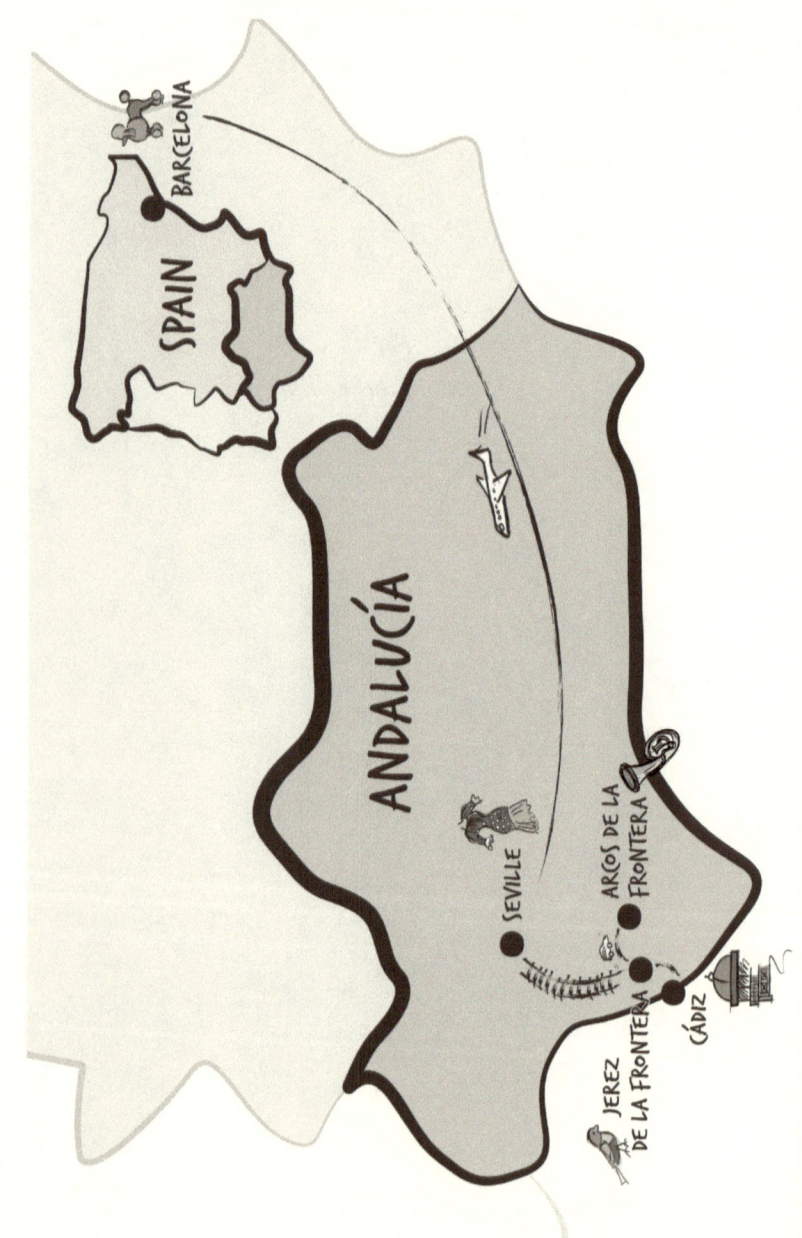

1

LA INICIACIÓN
The Point of No Return

Emilio Estévez changed my life.

When the epic western movie *Young Guns II* first premiered in Australia, I became so infatuated with Emilio's boyish good looks that – apart from plastering every square inch of my bedroom with his image and becoming the world's foremost expert on his cinematic career – I dedicated my graduating high school yearbook photo to him, with the ingeniously titled caption "*Emilio Lives!*".

Emilio's cheeky and charismatic portrayal of Billy the Kid amidst the romantic imagery of the American Southwest had such a profound and lasting effect on me that, several years later, I travelled solo throughout Arizona and New Mexico in the footsteps of the real Billy the Kid. (I may or may not have driven around Los Angeles hoping to bump into the real Emilio, too.) The most enduring legacy that captured my heart and refused to let go, however, was the haunting Spanish-sounding acoustic guitar featured throughout the film's soundtrack (even if it turned out to be more Mexican in the end).

On my return to Australia, I happened to catch the end of a televised dance special and became instantly transfixed as a Spanish *bailaora*, draped in a gloriously frilly dress, became hypnotically possessed by the wild, frenzied rhythms emanating from her flamenco guitarists; her twirling, graceful upper body movements starkly at odds with feet that hammered ferociously below. How had I not known about this before?! A perfectly legitimate and publicly acceptable social outlet for not only a hot-blooded, but a hot-headed woman to express herself to music that reminded her of Emilio Estévez?! The very next day, I signed up to the one and only flamenco class I could find in Brisbane.

Fascinatingly, whilst flamenco comes under the broad umbrella of Latin music, it has nothing to do with the *salsa*, the *samba*, the *merengue* or the *lambada*. You need neither a partner nor a slinky costume to dance it; nor is it a dance style you can grasp the basics of in an hour, then bump and grind your way around a room like you're Ricky Martin. As a beginner, if it feels awkward, alien and discombobulating then – trust me – you're doing it correctly.

Only if you persevere through the aching wrists, swollen feet and eccentric rhythms, an intoxicating new landscape of passionate, full-bodied expression awaits. Although the steps and rhythms become exponentially more complex, once you've fallen into flamenco's seductive grasp there is absolutely no escape. You will become a member of this evocative and mysterious club for life, devoting every waking hour to discovering its profound, sacred depths – and still only ever scratch the surface.

With precious few flamenco teachers in Australia when I was starting out (particularly of the male persuasion), one of the most breathlessly anticipated highlights of the year was when a touring artist held a dance workshop in town. The very first of these masterclasses was run by Antonio Vargas, the flamenco dancer who played Fran's father in the Australian film *Strictly Ballroom*. Although I was an absolute novice at the time, just to be in the same room as such a magnificent *maestro* (and his bouffant hair) was worth the price of admission alone.

So, too, the rare time an international show toured Australia, every flamenco student within a 500-kilometre radius would be in attendance trying to absorb as much of the authentic *aire* – or infectious energy – as was humanly possible. One of the most memorable performances was staged by a lively bunch of *gitanos*, who admirably shunned fancy costumes and elaborate production values in favour of their own raw, honest interpretation. The leader of the dance pack was a diminutive firecracker of a woman who left us rather gobsmacked when it became evident she danced without any knickers on. Every time she spun around, we would shout, '*Arsa!*' – a flamenco call that roughly, and most appropriately, translates to 'Show us your bits!'.

Unrequited nudity aside, one of the most popular flamenco artists ever to have graced Australian shores has been Paco Peña, one of Spain's most treasured guitarists. Bless his cotton socks, for every few years Paco brings his troupe's latest production down under and remains the only international flamenco performer to consistently include Brisbane in his itinerary.

No one could ever forget their first Paco show. With just a few years of flamenco dance lessons under our belts, my friend Evie and I sat excitedly in the centre of Brisbane's opulent Concert Hall. Built specifically for live orchestral music, with every detail strategically designed to maximise acoustics, it was, as they say, a rather classy joint. Towering organ pipes soared above a romantically lit wooden stage, as plush illumination cast a glow of warm, rosy light across the auditorium. Evie and I had chosen seats just low enough to gaze up at a level of mastery we'd only dared dream of, and just far enough back to be able to see the all-important footwork.

When the theatre doors closed, a revered hush descended upon the capacity crowd as Paco, his fellow guitarists, singers and percussionist filed onstage. Then, with a seasoned nod to one another, the band burst into its first lively instrumental. For the second piece, an elegant female dancer glided serenely across the stage, sensually coiling her long, languid arms and slender wrists. She was followed by a young male *bailaor* whose sharp, modern style was imbued with a more classical background.

Lastly, a tall, sturdy stallion of a man with dark, wavy hair and a stubble-infused jaw strode out to join his contemporaries. Radiating equal measures of confidence and charm, he immediately commanded the stage with his masculine prowess. For his first dramatic solo, he performed a *martinete*: an intense song of lament. The stirring cadence of the music and the rising passion he evoked – peppered with explosive, fiery footwork – held the audience in a state of baited breathlessness and ardent anticipation. Personally, I couldn't take my eyes off his muscular thighs. I didn't know they made legs like that.

Just when the crowd couldn't take any more, or expect that the dancer had anything left in him, Señor Stud Muffin cranked it up another notch and played with us like *churros* in chocolate. At the end of his first number, when women in the audience were ready to throw their firstborn children at him, the appropriately named Ángel turned his back to us and cheekily lifted his jacket so we could appreciate his sublime buttocks. (Straight male audience members may just have remembered the music.)

Not only was Ángel a gorgeous international flamenco superstar who performed all over the globe, as I later discovered, but he also taught workshops to aspiring (and perspiring) dance students – the highlight of which was a week-long intensive held at the Festival de Jerez in southern Spain every year.

Whether he was performing a fun-loving *alegría* or a powerfully hypnotic *farruca*, Ángel's star burned ferociously and brilliantly. Halfway through his final solo, however, the hairs on the back of my neck stood up as if to say, *'Pay attention! Something important is about to happen!'* As the music gathered pace, I obediently watched wide-eyed as Ángel suddenly stopped in his tracks and raised his arm. His intense gaze followed the trajectory of his outstretched finger as he drew an imaginary line across the crowd until it landed on its final resting place – pointing directly at me.

It was all the encouragement I needed.

I was going to Spain.

2

LA LLAMADA
The Call

Over the following years (once a pre-booked trip to the United States with my mother was out of the way), I obsessively saved every cent to turn my flamenco dreams into reality and was over the moon when I finally booked a coveted spot in Ángel's dance workshop for the upcoming Festival de Jerez.

When Paco Peña announced he was to tour Australia a few months before the festival kicked off, a devilishly genius idea sprung to mind: what if I asked Ángel to teach a workshop in Brisbane on his days off? I simply couldn't wait any longer to learn from such an *extraordinario* physique.

I found contact details for Ángel's manager, Felipe, on Ángel's official website. The problem was, there was only a phone number listed – no email, which meant phoning a stranger in a foreign land and attempting to converse in a language I had no grasp of in order to ask a very big favour of his star protégé. On the assumption that Felipe wouldn't speak any English, I had written out a few carefully constructed questions in his native tongue.

Ring ring. Ring ring.

My heart raced out of control.

Ring ring. Ring ring.

My mouth was uncomfortably dry.

Ring ring. Ring ring.

What the hell was I doing?!

Click.

Suddenly, I was connected. A lady's voice echoed throughout the receiver: '*Lalalalalalalalala lalalalalala*' (or words to that effect). Then I was abruptly disconnected.

Either I had dialled the wrong number, or Felipe's wife was telling me off for having called at some ungodly hour that I had anticipated being a little godlier. I wanted to crawl under my blanket and forget about the whole thing until I imagined what it would be like to be in the same room as Ángel's thighs. I picked up the handset and dialled a little more correctly.

Ring ring. Ring ring.

'*Este es Felipe.*'

Holy #@$%!

'Ah um … hello! I mean *hola*, Felipe. *Me llamo* Stacey. I am calling you um … *de* Australia! Ah … *lo siento, no hablo español. Habla inglés?*'

'*Sí*. I speak English. Hello to you.'

A little colour returned to my face.

'Oh great! Um, hi there! I'm a flamenco student calling from Australia. I see um that Paco Peña is touring here soon and um …' I cleared my throat. 'Does that mean Ángel will be as well?'

'Jes, they will both be going to Australia.'

Oxygen began returning to my vital parts.

'Fantastic! Um, Felipe, I was just wondering, because we don't get many big name flamenco artists around here, do you think it might be possible for Ángel to maybe teach a workshop whilst he's in Brisbane?'

Silencio.

'I can set the whole thing up but I was just wondering what the chances were in the first place?' I asked hopefully.

'Mm. What was your name, sorry?'

'Stacey.'

'Eh-Stacey. *No sé.* Sorry, Eh-Stacey, I don't know. It is too early to know his … um, how you say … *calendario* … *agenda*. Ángel may not have ze time. He may not have many dayz off. Eh-Stacey, please can you zend me an email with your question? I will look at zis for you.'

It was all I could have done not to go into a coma.

'Thank you so much, Felipe!' I gushed after copying down his contact details. '*Muchas gracias* for your time. I am very grateful and happy we talked.'

'*De nada*, Eh-Stacey. Thank you for calling. Bye-bye.'

There wasn't a moment to waste. I jumped online and immediately sent off a professional-sounding request that I hoped disguised how excited I was at the possibility of such a dream coming true. A couple of days later there was no response, so I sent another email asking Felipe if he'd received my original message. Still no response. Not to be deterred, I resent the original email from a different account.

Success! Felipe replied and thanked me for my interest/obsession. He explained he had just spoken about the idea with Ángel but since he had such a jam-packed and demanding Australian tour schedule coming up, it wasn't going to be possible. I was crushed.

Several months later, on the eve of Paco's Brisbane show, I arrived uncharacteristically early and happened to see none other than the divine Ángel puffing away on a sneaky cigarette outside the venue. There was only one thing to do.

'Ángel!' I pounced. 'Sorry for the interruption. Um, *soy* Eh-Stacey! It's me! The girl who wanted you to teach a workshop here in Brisbane!'

After an agonising pause, a relieved look of recognition swept over Ángel's magnificent features and, in broken English, he apologised for not having had the time.

'Not your fault! You busy touring!' I gesticulated wildly to make up for my sudden inability to speak English. 'But we, the local flamenco students, we very happy because tonight, we watch you perform!'

Ángel stubbed out his cigarette and laughed. He was seconds away from disappearing backstage, so I launched my final assault.

'Um, Ángel, next year … ah next *año*, um … the Festival de Jerez? I go there. I go to Spain and next year at the Festival de Jerez, I learn from you!'

Ángel broke into a huge grin and planted a kiss on both my cheeks (on my face, sadly).

'*Bien*. I hope I zee you zen.' He smiled and, with a wink, he was gone.

3

ENTRADA ESPECTACULAR
How to Make an Entrance

I'm not the most punctual of travellers. On one of my first trips overseas, I missed six flights out of a possible 16. Who knew flying just down the road from Los Angeles to Mexico was considered international and required a check-in three hours beforehand?! When it finally came time to travel to Spain to see Ángel, I still hadn't learnt my lesson and became so distracted by the sumptuous aromas of a saucy stir-fry on the way to the international boarding gate, my trusty takeaway and I made the plane out of Brisbane with just seconds to spare – but at least I was the only passenger on board who enjoyed their in-flight meal.

Thirty hours of travel, eight hours of transit and two hours of sleep later, I arrived in Barcelona.

Whilst I had technically visited Spain before, I don't think viewing it from a Trafalgar tour bus that hurtled through 12 countries and a smorgasbord of cultures in 26 days at the speed of light really counted. Foggy recollections from having spent just four days in *España* in 1999 were limited to a few spicy highlights: a zesty *paella* in Toledo, a heated argument with my roommate in Zaragoza, using self-defence to fend off pickpockets in Barcelona and having to form a human chain with my fellow tour passengers in Madrid to pass our luggage along piece by piece so it wouldn't get stolen. Another tour company wasn't so lucky. As its passengers tucked into the breakfast buffet, most of the group's belongings were pinched straight off the bus.

That was the thing. In my travelling naiveté, I'd always imagined the worst cliché possible when it came to the appearance of pickpockets (i.e. a little bit rough around the edges), but when I first visited Barcelona in 1999, the brazen thieves that tried to rob me by shoving a piece of cardboard under my chin, whilst another went behind to rummage through my backpack were young, hip girls that looked like they'd stepped straight out of a Wham! video clip – a pair of careless friskers, if you would.

(Please understand I have no issues with *gitanos*, or anyone from the much-maligned *Romaní* community. There are about 1 million residing in Spain alone and, without them and their incredibly resilient and dynamic culture, flamenco – at the very least – would not and could not exist. I have just always preferred it if someone would break into a *bulería* rather than my handbag.)

Ten years after my first visit, Barcelona was still considered the pickpocket capital of the world (hurrah!) as thieves employed a whole new manner of creative endeavours to get their hands on everyone's cash: they blocked train doors, they bumped into you, they felt you up, they asked you for directions, they hurled a fake baby at you or threw what smelled like bird poop at you and offered to take you to their nearby home to get cleaned up and/or cleaned out.

With clueless foreigners being the most lucrative targets, it was crucial to pretend you were a local at all times; a great idea in theory but when you were weighed down by a backpack the size of a minibus, other tactics were forced to come into play. In order to outwit potential thieves at the Barcelona Airport, I decided to glare angrily at everyone in the terminal – babies and children included. I was so hard core, I didn't even use the complimentary luggage trolleys, preferring to stubbornly stagger along with the weight of the world on my shoulders, fuelled by nothing but fury and pride.

'Flamenco is not about looking pretty,' a visiting instructor told our class once. 'Your face should reflect the intense emotions your body is feeling and the music conveying.' Naturally, the teacher was perpetually perplexed as to how anyone learning such a passionate, all-encompassing art form could ever dance with a poker face. His comments resonated so much, I threw everything I had into expressing myself completely from then on. Unfortunately, not all of my classmates got the memo and for a couple of years there my *gesto*, or flamenco face, was a source of great amusement. But I'd rather look frank than blank any day.

Thanks to my imposing scowl at the Barcelona Airport, not a single commuter or canny thief came within foraging distance of me. There was only one hitch in my cunning plan: I had yet to buy a train ticket into town. A 10-trip fare was, by far, the most enticing and inexpensive option available – it was just extracting money from a zipped pocket at the front of my trousers at the adjoining train station without attracting any attention that was the challenge. As I cautiously purchased a pass from one of the automatic ticket machines, I couldn't help but notice a group of young American girls nearby struggling to complete the same task. I reticently offered assistance only when I could no longer stand their overt *incompetencia*.

Finally, when both my change and train ticket appeared to be safely tucked away, I hobbled onto the crowded platform just as the city-bound train was approaching. Jostling for position, I was forced to manoeuvre into incredible feats of *contorsión* just to fit my backpack through the train doors. Once I'd collapsed onto the only vacant seat left in the carriage, an amorous couple – whom I'd already spotted going for it on the platform – locked lips the entire journey into town. If they were pickpockets practising the art of distraction, they were rather good.

Before I'd left home, a guitarist friend of mine had given me the business card of a *pensión* he recommended situated in the older part of Barcelona. Leaving nothing to chance, I had printed out an online map of the immediate surrounds. According to the digital directions, the closest train station to the *pensión* was Estació de França.

When I arrived, the relief at not only finding the correct station but no longer having to listen to saliva being exchanged in front of me was palpable. I stumbled onto the platform in search of the exit, before I realised with horror that my train ticket had gone missing. What on earth had I done with it?!

Had the American girls been international pickpockets in disguise? Then it hit me. Before boarding the train, I'd ever so briefly popped the ticket into my jacket pocket ready for when I disembarked but I'd been so busy trying to glare at everyone, balance my backpack and ignore the public displays of lust to notice it had vanished.

There was no way through the automatic exit at Estació de França without a ticket and, with no staff around to plead my case to, I threw my backpack on the ground and started searching in vain. Just as I was doing so, a security guard and his dog patrolled past.

'*Por favor!*' I leapt to my feet. 'No ticket! *Yo no ticketo! Pickpocketos!* Ticket … *vamos!*'

Thanks to my appalling grasp of their language, the old man and his dog looked at me with a mixture of pity and bemusement before graciously allowing me to depart the station for free.

'*Gracias! Muchas gracias!*' I gushed as my backpack and I scuttled towards the exit.

Once outside the train station, it was rather disconcerting to note the actual street view was exceedingly different from the virtual street view I had printed out – in that there was no similarity whatsoever. Hiking around the perimeter of the train station offered no further clues. Just as I was about to start conjuring up profanities, an office worker rushed past on her way home.

'*Perdón, Señora!*' I threw myself in her path. '*Por favor! Bitte hilf mir!* I'm lost!' I pressed the *pensión's* business card into her hand. '*Inglés? Habla inglés?*' I asked in anticipation.

The woman shook her head and motioned her boyfriend over. After furrowing his brow at both my exclamations and the business card, he suddenly had a brainwave: he pulled out his phone and rang the *pensión* for directions. *Estupendo!* I would have kissed him if he wasn't so tall, or taken.

In broken English, my saviour informed me that I was actually at Clot Station (*Excuse me?!*) and that I should travel to La Something or Other Station, where I should change trains before disembarking at Barceloneta Station. As I walked back to reunite with the security guard and his dog, I flipped the business card over for the first time. There, on the back, was a concise map with directions on how to find the *pensión* from Barceloneta, the nearest train station.

Hindsight was a wonderful thing.

When I was finally on my way to La Something or Other Station, with a second newly purchased 10-trip ticket in hand, I noticed a group of teenage girls at the other end of the carriage blatantly laughing at me. Surely there was nothing amusing about a curvy, dishevelled, hungry and exhausted *turista* who had recently and accidentally received the shortest haircut of her life before leaving Australia that resulted in a chic, too ahead-of-its-time, balding pixie hairdo?! Nevertheless, the snickering continued until I changed trains.

I left the safety of the train carriage only when I was absolutely certain I was at Barceloneta Station and hadn't inadvertently travelled to France. The map on the back of the business card made it very clear I should go straight, but when I ascended to street level, there were four kinds of straight to choose from. It was already well past my dinner time and I was getting, what some would say, a little shirty. With jetlagged instincts, I chose the street that looked the most right (actually it went left, but it was impressively dark and streety) and trekked about a kilometre until I found a corner store. Naturally, the shop owner had never heard of the mysterious *pensión* and, after a brief animated *discusión* with several customers, I was pointed vaguely in the direction I had just come from.

'*Gracias,*' I volunteered through gritted teeth and returned to pound the pavement, shuffling aimlessly alongside some kind of waterway in a fatigued stupor until I finally recognised a street from the map. Several blocks later, tucked down a little laneway, I found the *pensión*! Additional excitement abounded when I discovered there were no lifts to the reception located on the third floor. Several urgent rings of the reception bell later and I was all paid up for the night, before being pleasantly surprised to find that my room was located an additional two flights above. *Maravilloso.*

Stepping inside my new digs was like stuffing myself into an oversized wardrobe. There was just enough space to open the door ajar before I tripped over a single bed, but at least without any pickpockets around, I wouldn't have to look so cranky anymore.

As I unfastened the strap from around my waist and hoisted the backpack off my shoulders, my trousers followed suit and fell to the floor. It was only then that I realised, with horror, that I had been a walking peep show all afternoon, thanks to the waist strap of my backpack having undone not only my belt buckle but my fly as well – exposing my undies to all and sundry. At least it wasn't just my haircut the teenagers on the train had found so amusing.

It was past 8:30 p.m. and I was about to break my two cardinal rules of travelling:

1) Don't go out at night on your own.
2) Avoid olives at any cost.

The thought of even more meandering to find any kind of sustenance conflicted with my innate fear of eating out on my own, at night, in a country I barely spoke or read the language of, when all I really wanted to do was blend into the background and not be a travelling freak show for the evening. In the end, hunger won out over vanity.

When he could tear himself away from his incessantly loud television, the man at reception recommended a great restaurant just down the road – or at least that's what I thought he said. Wherever I ended up, I knew I could order at least one thing with absolute confidence – *la cerveza* – but being that I despised beer and was allergic to the gluten in it, it wasn't going to be the best opener.*

Directly across from the *pensión* was a fabulously crowded, standing-room-only *tapas* bar filled with fashionably stylish people all shouting at one another. Asking abundant questions

---

* Disclaimer: I don't eschew wheat, barley or rye to annoy restaurateurs, friends or to send bakeries bankrupt. When some well-meaning moron says, 'It's only got a little bit of gluten in it,' I want to slap them into next Sunday with a stale baguette. 'It's a medical condition, not a lifestyle choice!' I want to scream. Still, there's nothing like dietary restrictions to spice up one's travels.

about *trigo*, or wheat, were not going to go down, or be heard, too well so I pressed on.

A few schmancy restaurants, an empty Irish pub, a Japanese fine dining outlet and countless blocks later, I found the dodgiest, smokiest, most homely-looking bar on the strip and checked my fly before venturing inside.

'*Quiero un vino tinto, por favor,*' I declared. The barman showed me a bottle of red. 'No, no.' I waved my hands. 'Only one. Just one glass, please.'

'*Un vaso?*'

'Oh um … *sí*.' If there was ever an occasion to indulge in a vase of red wine, surely that had to be it. Standard alcoholic measures were rendered obsolete as the barman filled my glass to the brim.

'*Y una tortilla, por favor.*' It was the only item I recognised from the menu.

'*Una tortilla entera? O un trozo?*' The barman mimed an enormous plate followed by a small triangle.

'Oh sorry. *Un trozo, por favor.*' It was encouraging the barman had enough faith in me to be able to polish off an entire *tortilla* and bottle of wine in one sitting though. Contented that I had humiliated myself enough for the day, I retreated to a nearby table. A few moments later, a complimentary plate of detestable green olives arrived. The moment of truth: would I pass out from hunger or accept such generous hospitality? I winced through two and a half of the odious orbs from hell before my gag reflex kicked in. To this day, it is the greatest compliment I have ever bestowed upon a country and its cuisine.

It wasn't long before the local drunk made an appearance and collapsed at the table opposite me, trying in vain to convince his revolving eyeballs to focus on either the sports game blaring from the television above, or the one and only poker machine in the joint. I gave him a brief nod before pondering whether to offer him the rest of my olives. As I sat and waited for anything resembling food to arrive, it took all of my strength not to start gnawing on one of the huge legs of *jamón serrano* hanging above the bar.

Since having given up eating most types of meat as a teenager, I had been quasi-faux vegetarian, in that I had been eating chicken and fish for several years hoping that they didn't actually count (whoops!). But as my fatigue levels became preposterously and permanently low, I was medically ill-advised to consider being carnivorous again (spoiler alert: it didn't work). As an experiment, or more to appease gluten-loving friends who'd given up on inviting me over for dinner, I'd decided to give gnawing on animal carcasses one more go and had planned the trip to Spain to coincide with My Year of Eating Meat – in the hope that the offcuts of any long-departed creatures weren't also coated in a layer of gluten.

Just as my *tortilla* arrived so, too, did an elderly couple with their poodle. Somehow, the pampered pooch managed to spy my dinner through the plumes of cigarette smoke and proceeded to stare unblinkingly at me as I inhaled the omelette – and the passive equivalent of two hits of tobacco – in one go.

Pokies, poodles, puffers and pork? Barcelona was my kind of place.

4

SIN SUERTE
Out of Luck

Fortuitously or foolishly, my first full day in Spain fell on Friday the 13th but luckily there was no need to avoid black cats balancing on ladders since Hispanics and Greeks observed an entirely different day: that of Tuesday the 13th. (At least everyone agreed on the number 13 as being inauspicious.) Daring to be different, Italians claimed to be the only country that feared Friday the 17th. They also dedicated the second day of November to honouring their deceased, but if that same month also happened to include a freaky Friday the 17th, then look out: the entire *month* of November could be devoted to their grateful dead.

In Spain, there's a great saying of '*Martes, ni te cases ni te embarques*' that roughly translates to 'Tuesdays, don't get married or embark (on a boat)'. Poor unfortunate souls who suffer from *trezidavomartiofobia* – or fear of Tuesday the 13th – take it one step further: every Tuesday the 13th they refuse not only to get hitched, but shun every mode of transport by not leaving their house for 24 hours. That's commitment.

With no self-respectable train in Barcelona operating in the early mornings, I was thankful there would at least be no more undressing-on-public-transport rites of passage on the way to the airport. Instead, the *pensión's* receptionist had kindly pre-booked a taxi for me. After my brief overnight stay in Barcelona, I was on my way to the southern city of Seville where I had enrolled at a prestigious dance academy for the fortnight, before heading off to Jerez for its annual flamenco festival – and the very long-awaited workshop with Ángel.

'*De dónde eres?*' the friendly, middle-aged taxi driver enquired.

'*Australia,*' I replied, hoping I had comprehended the question correctly.

'*Australia?!*' she exclaimed. '*Estás aquí de vacaciones?*'

All I understood was the holiday part. 'Um, sort of. I'm here to learn flamenco. Ah ... *yo aquí por flamenco.*'

'*Flamenco?!*' The driver looked me up and down before returning her gaze to the road. Clearly she had never encountered a pale, frazzled, short-haired, too-tight pant-wearing Australian *guapa* in her taxi before. '*Eres bailaora de flamenco?*' she asked, mouth agape.

'*Sí.* Well kind of. I'm more of a student over here. *Estudiante,*' I proposed and the driver visibly relaxed. She then let me in on a little secret. Even though she lived in Barcelona and regarded it to be a great city, she believed Seville to be truly beautiful. The fact that I would be studying such a passionate art form in such picturesque surrounds would make it even more enchanting, she affirmed.

As we pulled up outside the Barcelona Airport, the driver cautioned me to be extremely on guard the second I left her taxi as there were many pickpockets about. She then graciously lightened my load by charging an exorbitant tariff; immediately reducing my financial appeal to future assailants who were, fortunately, still thin on the ground.

Once my backpack and I were safely checked in, with pockets zipped up and a filthy scowl plastered on my face, I power-walked over to the food court in search of *desayuno*. Despite my protestations of '*No puedo comer trigo*' – aka 'Gluten gives me gas' – there was nothing but a bounty of bakery products on offer, save for one little slice of *tortilla* that, once again, saved my proverbial bacon.

The flight from Barcelona to Seville was a cosy affair, packed with native Spaniards who, like me, were outraged at having to be up before the sun – assuming they'd even been to bed in the first place. Not long into our ascent, I regretted wolfing down the greasy *tortilla* so close to boarding such a budget aircraft throughout which oxygen appeared to be in short supply. Clutching a sick bag, I watched as the Spanish air hostesses tried to flog their overpriced drinks, before they sat down and gasbagged for the rest of the journey. It was the only in-flight entertainment on offer.

It seemed far too early for pickpockets to be casing the airport in Seville but I exhibited extreme signs of paranoid animosity just in case. Months of meticulous research had determined exactly how and where I would catch the local bus into town (my wallet couldn't handle another taxi), and I was pretty chuffed when I was the first in line at the bus stop. Ten minutes later, a truckload of travellers with the same intention suddenly appeared and I soon found myself pushed to the back of the queue. When the Seville-bound bus finally showed up half a day later, I had the correct change all ready to go, but since the fares had inadvertently increased by €0.40 since I'd last checked them online, I was forced to scramble through my pockets to make up the shortfall.

Seville was still shaking off its slumber as the bus approached; its myriad apartment buildings were being gently roused by the sun's blossoming rays. As we glided through pleasant, wide tree-lined streets, I was impressed with the abundant fountains and scenic gardens about the place until, 30 minutes later, the bus driver abruptly pulled over, turned the motor off and exited the coach, leaving a handful of confounded passengers in his wake. It took each one of us a full five minutes before we realised the random, non-descript, middle-of-nowhere bus stop was as close to the centre of Seville as we were ever going to get.

By the time my backpack and I exited the bus, my fellow commuters had all but vanished and I instantly regretted not availing myself of one of the free maps at the airport, fearful of drawing any unnecessary attention to myself. Really, it was a bit late for that. I was clearly and self-consciously the only tourist for miles. With no other choice, I started dragging myself towards where I hoped the centre of town was. When that grew old, I plucked up the courage to ask a local for assistance, only to acutely recall I hadn't yet had time to learn any Spanish directional phrases – and ended up adding a gruelling 20 minutes to my already extended trek.

At last when I arrived at my hotel, I was crushed to discover none of the reception staff could, or would, speak English. Fortunately, I had already written out a page of relevant phrases; it was just unfortunate none of us could read my scratchy handwriting. Eventually, with key in hand, I made my way up to my very own little Spanish sanctuary located on the first floor, where the biggest welcome basket of glutenous goodies you could ever imagine was waiting for me. I was touched.

I'd meticulously chosen the hotel due to its location in Triana: a charming little *barrio*, or neighbourhood, across the river from Seville's city centre. It was also home to the dance academy I had enrolled in for the fortnight.

For pretty much an eternity, Triana was regarded as THE thriving *gitano* neighbourhood of Seville until the 1960s and '70s when the local council decided to "relocate" all of the long-term residents – in the most heavy-handed way possible – to the outskirts of town and subsequently charge higher rents to the *payos*, or non-*gitanos*, who moved in. A god-awful eyesore of a squalid apartment wasteland known as Las Tres Mil was one such slum built for the persecuted *gitanos*, where many remained in dire straits today. There was nothing like sweeping an entire vibrant culture under the proverbial rug to try and deal with a situation, was there? At least no one could ever take flamenco away from them.

In my haphazard journey to the hotel, I'd spied a convenience store on the outskirts of Triana and decided to make my way back there in search of *mucha agua*. (Being the proud owner of the world's most delicate constitution, tap water from just an hour south of where I lived could churn my stomach.) Finally, with two cumbersome 5-litre bottles of water balanced in each hand, I took what appeared to be a shortcut back to the hotel, only to come across a very large SuperSol grocery store *diagonally across the road* from where I was staying.

A wonderfully similar moment occurred on the previous trip to America when I experienced a classic sitcom moment after I bent down to pick something up off the floor and heard a loud CRACK that rendered me unable to stand upright for the rest of the day. I then spent a fun-filled morning crouched over at the New York Public Library ringing every osteopath and chiropractor listed in the phone directory but, with no one able to understand my Aussie accent, everyone concluded I was *on* crack, rather than suffering from the effects of one. My poor mother, who was travelling with me for the first and, presumably, last time was forced to contend with carrying both of our heavy daypacks up and down the relentless subway stairs. It was only when we arrived back at our hotel that evening that I noticed a remedial massage centre *directly across the road*.

Back in Triana, I was desperate to get stuck into a packet of gluten-free noodles that had faithfully travelled all the way from Australia with me. After firing up the old electric stove in the kitchenette, I was thrilled to note each hotplate took a full 10 minutes just to reach room temperature. After 11 minutes, I'd had enough and ducked over to the nearby

SuperSol; the front of which housed a bakery dedicated to the most torturously delectable golden breads, pastries, cakes, biscuits and slices in existence. If only it was My Year of Eating Wheat.

The layout of the supermarket was ingeniously simple: each aisle was devoted purely to one type of foodstuff. There was a refrigerated cheese aisle, a dedicated tinned tomato aisle, a bottled anchovy aisle and, most disconcertingly, an insidious olive aisle. In the oil section, customers had a choice of local virgin, extra virgin and born-again varieties with their deep emerald nectars encased in huge glass *botellas*. I only needed a meagre excuse for sustenance to liven up my noodles, so I selected a few fresh, plump tomatoes and plonked them down on the conveyor belt, alongside a small bottle of olive oil. The shop assistant immediately glowered at me.

'*Hola?*' I offered with an uncertain smile.

Before I could commend her on her company's excellent floor plan, the check-out chick grabbed my tomatoes and disappeared. In her absence, a growing queue of tut-tutting housewives formed behind me. Before I could proclaim ignorance, the assistant returned with my three tomatoes luxuriating in a giant plastic bag. Determined not to affront any further local customs, I paid up and fled back to the hotel where I spent the next hour pondering whether the environment was of any concern to Spaniards, whilst waiting for the noodle water to boil.

5

FUERTE
Go Hard (or Go Home!)

'What the *diablo*?!'

It was 7:30 a.m. on a Saturday. Everyone in the country was sound asleep, except for some very loud-talking handymen in the room opposite mine – who were drilling and hammering up a storm as if their lives depended on it. It was, in short, an affront to Spain: land of the eternal night owls, where shops didn't open until mid-morning, *siestas* didn't kick off until mid-afternoon and families dined out late at night. On behalf of the nation, and all the other hotel guests, I decided to tackle the troublemaking tradies head-on with some good old-fashioned Aussie backbone but somehow in my post-noodle, bed-haired state, the phrase 'Don't-you-know-how-#@$%-early-it-is?!' came out as a feeble '*Hola*' after which my backbone and I fled back to bed.

'Meet me at the Puerta de Jerez fountain at midday?'

It was a text from my Aussie-Spanish friend Sebastian who'd moved to Seville a couple of years prior. Sebastian and I had studied dance together in Brisbane for many years, during which time he fell so hard for flamenco's beguiling charms, he devoted himself to listening to, and watching, as much of it as he could without being arrested.

Once, when fellow students and I were invited back to Sebastian's place after a weekend workshop, he had a DVD of his favourite dancer – Rafael Campallo – playing in the background, as the students and I collectively oohed and aahed over Sebastian's new crisp, white flamenco boots.

Dedicating himself to flamenco by night, whilst holding down an unfulfilling desk job by day, eventually wore Sebastian down and it wasn't long before he threw in his job, moved to Seville and took up dancing full-time.

'*Sí, see you there, guapo!*' I replied, relieved that the fountain Sebastian had chosen was just across the bridge from Triana.

Even in his native country, Sebastian was easy to spot. His tall, lean frame, olive skin and dark, shoulder-length hair were universal enough – as were his strong Latino features – but there was something about him; an inexplicable force that always and inevitably drew you in. On the outside, Sebastian appeared passionately driven and ambitious, but on the inside – he was a complete and utter softie – especially when it came to affairs of the heart. (He also had an unnerving interest in watching people have practical jokes played upon them.)

Sebastian was pacing back and forth when he spotted me. '*Guapa!* So good to see you!' He pulled me into a huge embrace before adding, 'You're late.'

'For what?!' I hadn't realised we were already on a schedule.

'My friend is performing right now! We gotta go!' And with that, he grabbed my arm and broke into a run. Sebastian's Italian friend Mateo – who also happened to be the only other straight man in his dance class – was busking in the Plaza del Triunfo with his flamenco troupe. To get there, Sebastian and I sprinted past the third largest cathedral in the world, leapt over a tram line, dashed past countless cafés and bars and hurried past carriage-pulling horses enjoying refuge in the shade before we arrived at the plaza. It was like sightseeing on speed.

We heard them before we saw them. The sharp *ratatata* of nail-infused heels, a young woman's plaintive cry and the rich, melodic strains of the guitar reverberated throughout the square.

'Keep your bag close, Stace. There'll be pickpockets about,' Sebastian warned as we snaked our way towards the front of the swelling crowd. After living so long in Seville, Sebastian still had to be vigilant every day.

A young man dressed as a poetry major – complete with spectacles and a beret – was bashing out a driving rhythm on the *cajón*, or box drum. The female singer's face was contorted with anguish as she channelled the grief of her ancestors; her black Converse shoes tapping in time to the stirring music. To save money on chairs, two male guitarists clad in jeans, T-shirts and work boots were perched on the ledge of an ornate sandstone building behind the stage. A small speaker balanced precariously on top of a wheelie bin whilst directly in front, an upturned black hat loitered for donations. Good luck to anyone who managed to extract cash from their pockets without being targeted as a human vending machine, I figured.

Ratatatata.

As a young female dancer took to the stage in billowing polka-dot sleeves and a long, black skirt, I watched in wide-eyed wonder as her feet began hammering out rhythmic patterns on the makeshift dance floor – two wooden tabletops bound together with masking tape. By her side was Mateo, who was feverishly clapping his cadenced support. As the dancer's momentum intensified, her tousled raven hair began to unravel as her flamenco shoes slammed harder and faster onto the tabletops. '*Olé!*' someone cried out as the music accelerated, taking everyone's pulses along with it.

'*Vamos ya!*' Let's go! The guitarists' fingers were strumming like they were on fire, whilst the hands of the *cajón* player were fast becoming indistinguishable from one another. '*Venga, chica!*' Come on, girl! *Ratatatata*. Sweat was pouring down the dancer's face as the midday sun beat down upon her neck. Then, with arms extended to the heavens, she executed her final *remate* and launched into a triumphant finish. '*Olé, guapa!*' The crowd exploded with cheers, applause and wolf whistles. Sebastian snuck me a mischievous smile.

Only someone with true *cojones* (no relation to the drum) could have followed, and the striking Mateo was the perfect man for the job. With a liberal sprinkling of cheekiness and sass, he unleashed a much more modern interpretation upon the unsuspecting crowd. Writhing around in a frenzy, perfectly attired in his rock star black shirt, tight black trousers and boots, Mateo busted out so many hip thrusts and wiggles, I think he may have been a stripper back in Italy.

Mateo and Sebastian had one of the most acclaimed flamenco schools in Seville to thank for honing their exemplary skills: the Academia de Flamenco Manuel Betanzos. After listening to Sebastian wax so lyrically about Manuel and his teaching style since he'd arrived in Seville, I just had to experience it for myself.

Another dancer friend of mine had been similarly inspired to study at Manuel's. However, when she arrived in Triana, she became so overwhelmed by the magnitude of it all, it took her a good half hour just to pluck up the courage to face the academy. She approached the building three times before she could even put her hand on the front door, convinced she was not worthy of such an esteemed institute. I think the only reason she ended up going inside was because she was more embarrassed about some old biddy watching her antics from across the street than her own insecurities.

To avoid a similar scenario, after Mateo's show Sebastian kindly offered to show me where Manuel's illustrious dance studio was located and how to reach it from my hotel. As we strolled throughout Triana, Sebastian explained that dance students were most welcome to drop into any public flamenco class anywhere in Seville, to observe a lesson and see if a particular teacher and/or choreography were for them – a sort of a try before you cried, I guessed.

'You ready, Stace?' Sebastian asked as we stood before the towering wooden doors of Manuel's academy. The immense influence, significance and cultural impact of the dance school had begun with its founding director, Manolo Marín. Like many of his peers, the Seville-born Manolo started dancing as a young *niño*, before the mostly self-taught dancer started choreographing, performing and teaching for international theatre, film and television (including stints at the Paris and Cairo Operas, and Barcelona Olympics). Since he had flung open the doors to his esteemed academy, Manolo had nurtured the careers of many of the industry's most celebrated dancers and, even though he had officially retired from running the place, his wisdom and expertise were never too far away.

On the odd occasion he was asked to step in as a guest teacher, Marín defied his 70-odd years and would throw his heart and soul into the class, instructing for hours at a time in up to five different languages. The best part was, at the end of the lesson when the students performed his choreography, Manolo would yell, '*Jamón!*' meaning 'Ham it up!' and mockingly invite his protégés to busk for him under the Triana Bridge for a euro apiece.

'I'm ready, Seb.' I braced myself as we stepped into the inner sanctum of the academy. Incense and candles dotted the cosy timber interior and instantly melted away any apprehensions with their warm embrace. A kind, multilingual Japanese lady welcomed us at reception before an enticing hallway lit with ornate lamps beckoned us into its silhouetted depths. At the end of the passageway was the main *estudio*: a long, bright room with floor-to-ceiling mirrors, marbled walls, an adjacent courtyard and an elevated stage that featured the most exciting component of all – live musicians.

The afternoon class was in full swing, so Sebastian and I snuck in via the side and watched in silent awe as the female instructor imparted her expertise at breakneck speed. The pace and power of her footwork was so intense, the nail tips on the underside of the students' shoes had ripped the bottom of their practice skirts to shreds. The teacher's name was Adela Campallo, sister of Rafael – Sebastian's DVD flamenco hero. Since her professional debut at the age of nine, Adela had blazed an impressive solo career before a shocking car accident almost broke her in two. Her back had been so badly injured, flamenco was completely out of the question. Yet, only a handful of years later, she was defying all the odds. Her secret weapon? Until she was able to dance with her body, Adela had danced with her soul.

That was the thing about such an all-embracing art form – at the end of the day, no matter the teacher, the style, the training or the journey that had led you there, if you didn't dance every step with indefatigable passion and fire, it just wasn't flamenco.

At last I understood why my friend had been so hesitant to walk into Manuel's academy. It was all well and good flouncing around Brisbane doing a couple of advanced classes *per week* but in Spain, where I was well and truly considered a beginner, I somehow had to find the stamina to do two classes *per day* at one of the most highly regarded dance schools in Andalucía – the birthplace of flamenco, no less.

To ease my increasing anxieties, Sebastian invited me over to another student's house that evening for a "F@#% You Valentine's Day!" themed party. I'd completely forgotten it was the international day of love and, as sorely tempting as it would have been to descend into the ranks of dateless debauchery after just 24 hours in Seville, I regrettably declined; choosing instead to curl my weary bones up on my apartment's cow-print sofa and watch *Se Llama Copla*: Spain's answer to *Australian Idol*.

And people wondered why I was always single.

6

ZAPATEADO
A Whole Lot of Stomping Going On

My first official day at Manuel's academy started not with a bang but with a '#@$%!' as my trusty alarm clock slept in with me. Thunderous echoes of what sounded like a furniture moving party above the previous night hadn't helped matters either. With only half an hour to be dressed, fed and at the studio, I raced like the clappers. Sebastian had warned me how much Manuel abhorred tardiness and that it would be more respectful to skip an entire lesson than to ever be late. With just moments to spare, I threw myself into the academy's wooden entryway, hurled my belongings into the ladies' changing room and scurried into the studio, feeling like the Spanish equivalent of a fish out of water – or as the locals say – *'como un pulpo en un garaje'* (like an octopus in a garage).

As soon as Manuel entered the studio, I warmed to him immediately. His presence was as serene as it was commanding, accompanied by just a hint of a sparkle in his eyes. As he ran a sun-kissed hand over his closely shaven head, Manuel surveyed the room, taking note of any new recruits before he spun on his heels and faced the mirror.

'*Y!*' Manuel shouted as he grabbed the front of his shirt with his fist and pummelled the soles of his boots into the wooden floor. On the count of 'And!' our rapid-fire warm-up had begun and took no prisoners with its fervour or ferocity. The *palo*, or style, of song being taught in the first class was an *alegría* – one of my all-time favourites that literally meant happiness, which made it an absolute joy to ever watch or perform. The tricky steps the diminutive Manuel required the beginners to keep up with, however, quickly wiped the smile off my face.

Sebastian had let me in on a little secret: if Manuel paid you attention, he cared about you and your progress but if he ignored you, you should probably take up the Highland Fling. Manuel also had the uncanny ability to be aware of every single one of his 30 students, no matter where they were in the room, so there was never any point trying to hide up the back.

We were only halfway through the first class when it happened. Like an eagle-eyed moth to an insecure flame, just as we were drilling a particular marking step, Manuel appeared instantly by my side and put one hand on my sternum and the other on my upper back, before he actively pushed my torso up and forward. His accompanying words were, no doubt, equally profound and meaningful.

Unbeknownst to me, for almost a decade I had been dancing with a concave chest, a habit that had spread through to everyday life; hunching over so as not to draw any attention to myself (unless I was on stage, that was). It took Manuel only one class to correct the posture – and 170 more classes to make it a habit – but the significance of standing proud and holding myself with confidence, even with a bad haircut and self-doubting thighs, would continue to resonate for life.

The second class was an intermediate level *tiento* – a slower, more solemn style of dance. With my newfound self-assurance and tendency to make things harder for myself,* I managed to keep up with the complicated rhythms and offbeats whilst puffing my chest out like a peacock – at least for the first couple of minutes.

As stunning as Manuel's studios were, however, unfortunately they could not escape the scourge of inadequate plumbing that plagued the nation. Just as in many of the public restrooms around Seville, toilet paper was often to be deposited in a bin and not down the toilet. I had heard that was how it was in Greece due to its archaic pipes, but Spain? My meagre grasp of the language, combined with my sheer ignorance of the accompanying visual aids on the back of cubicle doors ensured it wasn't until my last few days in Spain that I finally followed the correct procedure, however grossly weird and disturbing that was.

Flamenco was an insatiable beast. I had just sweated, twirled and pounded my feet more in the past two hours

---

* By some stroke of genetic luck, I've always had a knack for being able to remember complex rhythms and patterns; it's just convincing my lower extremities to accurately reproduce them that is the dilemma.

than I collectively had in my life, yet I was hungry for more. It was with great delight then when I returned to my hotel and spotted another flamenco school *diagonally across the road* (there was a pattern forming). Surely it would have been most ungracious of me to have travelled so far and not attended classes at Isabel Bayón's academy as well? Besides, if I wanted to even remotely impress Ángel at the upcoming workshop in Jerez, it was *crucial* to get my flamenco fitness up to speed *pronto*. I hobbled up the stairs to the studio and signed up for one beginner's class per day for the rest of the week, effective immediately.

Isabel was away for a couple of days but had organised a guest teacher in her absence – none other than Rafael Campallo, the star of Sebastian's DVD collection. Rafa was absolutely everything you could ever want in a dancer: young, fit, cheeky and handsome. I just never got over the fact that, up close, he looked like a young Joe Pesci from the film *My Cousin Vinny*.

Over the subsequent hour, a handful of female students and I were to learn *pataitas y técnica por tangos* from the familiar-looking, lightning-footed *hombre*. Fortunately, Rafa kept the level of choreography fairly low, but when he encouraged us to repeat the simplest of steps at an agonisingly slow pace, we all began to stuff up royally. Eventually, when no one could even master the most basics of footwork due to overthinking every step, Rafa began to despair; as did I when all of my toes went completely numb for the first time in my life.

7

UN IDIOMA CONFUSO
Say What?!

Frankly, I was at a loss to explain how anyone with a pulse ever found the sitcom *Two and a Half Men* even vaguely amusing. I have nothing against the actors (Charlie Sheen is Emilio's brother after all), it's just the inane scriptwriters I'd have liked to slap around with a serrated rubber hose. Somehow, since its mindless inception, *Two and a Half Men* became so popular it ended up screening in over 40 countries. Whether all the exposure was really a covert marketing ploy to increase the sales of tenpin bowling shirts worldwide, I would never know, but *Dos Hombres y Medio* – even when comically dubbed into Spanish – still sucked.

Thank goodness for *Cifras y Letras* – or *Numbers and Letters* – the unconventional game show that tested intelligent, yet uncomfortable-looking contestants on their maths and spelling skills. Not only was it educational for viewers and contenders alike, no one needed to resort to overtly inappropriate sexual innuendo for the programme to be entertaining. It was also an ingenious way for hapless foreigners to increase their Spanish repertoire whilst they waited for their stoves to heat up.

Before I left Australia, I'd conned a colleague into lending me 60 hard-core conversational *castellano* audio lessons he had purchased. I managed only to get up to Lesson 12 before I blew an artery in my brain. With far too many syllables and elongated words to master, let alone fit into a sentence, I swiftly came to the conclusion that anyone who proclaimed Spanish (or, for that matter, flamenco) was easy to learn was a pathological liar.

You say, 'Nineteen'.

The Spanish declare, '*Diecinueve*' (*dee-es-ee-nweh-vay*).

Brits say, 'Left'.

Latinos exclaim, '*Izquierda*' (*iz-key-air-da*).

Nineteen, *diecinueve*, left, *izquierda* ...

It was rather tempting to call the whole thing off.

Even the simple act of parking a car can turn into an all-day event when you inform someone you're just popping off to the *estacionamiento* (*eh-sta-si-on-ah-me-en-toe*), or parking lot. Nobody has time for that!

In addition to all the syllables, depending on which region you are from, when a word ends in a 'z' or contains the letters 'ce', they can be pronounced with a 's' or a 'thw' sound, making it sound like you inadvertently have a gap in your front teeth the size of a Chihuahua.

Another linguistic tidbit that astonishes me is the fact that there are no native Spanish words beginning with a 'k' or 'w'. They simply do not exist! What if you were well keen to go wakeboarding with a Kit-Kat, a Wagon Wheel and

Kanye West (when he was known as such), or wanted to awaken Willy Wonka's knickers with a wedgie? You simply could not, well not in Spain or South America at any rate.

With two letters almost redundant from the Spanish alphabet, a couple more were added to boost numbers – and no doubt increase Scrabble scores – with the inclusion of double letters 'ch' and 'll' – the latter of which is pronounced as either a 'j' or a 'y'. However, in a shock move that no one saw coming, 'ch' and 'll' were officially thrown out of the Spanish alphabet by The Royal Spanish Academy in 2010, which immediately reduced the characters from 29 to 27. Only one hardy little guy survived the cull: the letter 'n' with a mini moustache on his head. Ladies and gentlemen, meet '*ñ*' – pronounced *'enye'* (like Enya, but with less reverb). Thanks to this jaunty little chap, you can enthusiastically exclaim notions such as *'Mañana, let's hit a piñata in España!'*

But be careful. Omitting him can have grave consequences. *'Yo tengo 36 años'* quite literally means *'I have 36 years* (of age)', but *'Yo tengo 36 anos'* means that you are, in fact, the proud owner of 36 anuses.

I have a shameful secret to confess. In addition to my inability to enjoy olives, I cannot for the life of me roll my 'r's. Over 400 million Spanish speakers across the globe somehow can, but for some reason my tongue has always refused to play ball. Since the addition of an extra 'r' can completely change the meaning of something, it sure makes for exhilarating times.

'Eso es bueno, pero' suggests 'That's good, but', whereas *'Eso es bueno, perro'* translates to 'That's good, dog'. (Really only

acceptable when conversing with your pooch.) '*Eso es caro*' informs a shop assistant something is expensive, whereas '*Eso es un carro*' explains that what you are looking at is, in fact, a car. (Of course, it's perfectly acceptable to ever speak up if you're sold a *carro* that's too *caro*.)

It would not be right, however, to proceed a millisecond further without addressing the proverbial *elefante* in the room.

¡¡What the freak is with all the extra Spanish punctuation marks!!

¿Isn't one exclamation or question mark enough per statement?

¿¡Without any full-stops at the *start* of sentences, why are '!' and '?' so freaking special?!

¿¡Are Spaniards such impatient readers that they need to know how each sentence is going to finish before they get to the end!?

¿What if a sentence contains both question and exclamation marks in it?

¡No hay problema!

¡You can put a different one at either end, can you believe that?

Mischievous punctuation marks can also sneak into the middle of a sentence ¡gosh darn it! No wonder Spaniards need a television show about their language.

A year after my return home, Australia began making its own version of *Numbers and Letters* but sadly, it was axed by some *anos* within a couple of *años*.

8

DIFÍCIL
The Opposite of Easy

'Complicado?' Manuel asked me with a knowing look. Tuesdays and Thursdays were notorious technique days that involved repeatedly practising intricate footwork patterns until Manuel was satisfied. The very first class nearly destroyed me both in complexity and temperature, with the studio mirrors fogging up from the warm-ups alone. At last I understood why Sebastian only went to one out of two technique classes per week.

Frustrated, I nodded back to Manuel determined not to let the relentless rhythms get the better of me. After two hours of toe-tapping torture, I was mentally kicking myself (as physically would have hurt too much) for paying for a whole week of classes at Isabel's studio as well. As much as I wanted to give Rafa's second class all of my energy and concentration, once he started jackhammering footwork, I was a goner. A spot of sightseeing would have been the perfect remedy to round the afternoon off but when your feet had been reduced to bloody stumps, sashaying about town was not an option.

When my guitarist friend first visited Seville, he'd rented a bike from the one of the public bike stations and recommended it as an ideal way to get around. Bear in mind, that advice came from the same friend who recommended the elusive *pensión* in Barcelona.

It was impossible for anyone to forget the name of Seville's bike rental company as Sevici was only a couple of letters away from *servicio*, or toilet. I figured they both offered a public service in their own way. Sevici had only been in business for a couple of years and had 2,500 bikes for rent but, much like the *pensión*, the fun part was trying to locate any of them. When you couldn't care less about cycling, you would inadvertently stumble across all 250 bike stations in Seville, but when you were in genuine need of hitting the pedal to the metal, good luck even finding a handlebar.

As I wasn't too keen on mime-asking the hotel reception staff where the nearest cycle station was, I jumped online at the nearby *cibercafé* and, lo and behold, there was a Sevici just around the corner. Better yet, there were three bikes available. The first half hour of any hire was free so, provided I actually knew where the next station was, I could technically scoot around town all afternoon, swapping bikes and never paying a *peso*. All I had to do was put my credit card into the pay station, slip into some Lycra and hey presto, I'd be doing the Tour de Seville in no time.

I was on the verge of forking out for a week's *bicicleta* hire at the automatic kiosk when I was brusquely informed there were no short-term facilities available at that payment post. I wasn't going to be in Seville for the long term, I tried to reason with the computer, unless someone proposed to me and I got married on a boat the following Tuesday. Repeating the instructions a second time elicited the same response, as did giving the computer stink-eye.

No matter. There was an exciting evening of entertainment afoot, just so long as I could drag myself there *on* foot. At Sebastian's insistence, I was off to one of Seville's most popular flamenco *tablaos*, or live flamenco venues. Locating a non-touristy *tablao* in Spain was a tricky affair. For the price of a plane ticket home, you could be enthralled by beautiful women in big frilly dresses with the equivalent of a bouquet of flowers on their heads, whilst guitarists paid tribute to the Gipsy Kings by playing endless *rumbas*. Or, if you knew the right places to go, you could find yourself dramatically plunged into the aching depths of flamenco's rousing heart and soul.

Flamenco is, by nature, a spontaneous expression of emotion. Within the structures of each *palo* there is scope for endless creativity and improvisation – an outward *manifestación* of the inner landscape, if you will. Some purists believe the formalisation and commercialisation of the art form is an affront to its fluid and impulsive spirit but think of how much richness, beauty – and hotness – the world would have missed out on if flamenco remained hidden in the shadows. There's no point having outrageous talent if you can't show it, and your knickers, off a little.

Just before the bridge out of Triana, I spotted another Sevici station and decided to give registration another go. As

I attempted to do so, a growing queue of passionate locals, impatient to secure one of the few remaining bikes, formed behind me. In the face of such mounting and dismounting pressure, I conceded defeat, cancelled my request and dragged myself into town.

'Attention! Attention!'

Startled, I looked around for the source of the sudden disruption. Scores of tourist boats were lined up along the edge of the Guadalquivir, hoping to entice passengers with their tacky brass music and cheesy, multilingual, bellowing voice-overs broadcast on a never-ending loop.

'Attention! Attention! This boat is leaving in one hour. Okay, let's go!'

I never saw a single passenger on any of the boats the entire time I was in Seville. Tourists just weren't used to being shouted at like that.

I was glad I had taken Sebastian's advice. The Casa de la Memoria, or House of Memories, was unquestionably the most picturesque flamenco venue imaginable. Tucked within the winding alleyways of the Barrio de Santa Cruz – the former Jewish quarter of Seville – the *tablao* was charmingly nestled within the candlelit courtyard of an 18th-century palace that was itself restored from a 15th-century Jewish house. It was impossible not to be swept up in the romance of it all as floral pots, lanterns and lush, green foliage adorned the overhanging balconies.

It was just gaining admittance that was the challenge.

Unlike more touristy offerings, the Casa de la Memoria was strictly a show-only affair. The venue offered neither an overpriced buffet nor an ostentatious wine list, which made it an outrageously popular night out.

When I arrived at the *tablao*, there was already an impressive queue of desperate and ticketless patrons lined up outside. Rumour had it that the 9 p.m. show was almost sold out. With only 80 seats available per performance, the odds certainly weren't in everyone's favour but, even when the *tablao* doors closed at 8:59 p.m., I refused to give up hope.

'*Hola! Hola! Tengo una entrada!* I have one ticket left!' the seller shouted from the box office.

'Can you squeeze two people in?' an Indian couple in front of me called out.

'No. Not two, only one.'

'What if we provide an extra chair?' they pleaded. You had to give them kudos for trying.

'No sorry. Please, the show is ready to go.'

'I'm on my own!' I sang out across the laneway. '*Yo sola!* I only need one seat!' The couple graciously gestured me towards the counter and, a mere €13 later, I was happily ensconced in the front row.

The star performer of the evening was Leonor Leal – a sassy, modern dancer acclaimed not only for her funky footwork and figure-hugging costumes, but for her short pixie haircut. Witnessing the flamenco equivalent of Pink in action sure made me feel a whole lot better about my own diminutive follicles. A singer, guitarist and male dancer – all of whom were young, supremely talented and ridiculously good-looking – completed the lineup.

Leonor danced two transfixing solos: a fiery, festive *bulería* followed by a sharp, powerful *farruca* (a dance that used to be the exclusive domain of men). Such was the charisma and enthusiasm of her shaggy-bearded, 21-year-old dance partner, all he had to do was look at audience members and they would erupt into a cheer.

By the time the highly engaging show wound up just after 10 p.m., the streets were teeming with people, which was in stark contrast to the deserted, tumbleweed-laden terrain of only a few hours prior. The later it was in Seville, the safer it seemed to feel. All around the plazas, couples walked hand in hand, tourists window-shopped and every child, parent, granny and dog were out enjoying dinner at one of the local bars. Everyone was so engrossed in their evening, no one noticed the street busker scratching out a badly tuned version of "Strangers in the Night" under the moonlit shade of an orange tree. So, too, when a large group of middle-aged men and women began rollerblading BACKWARDS throughout the main town square, no one even batted an eyelid.

It seemed Seville was going to take some getting used to.

9

SENTIMIENTOS DRAMÁTICOS
Express Yourself

I had started to notice an intriguing trend. Every time I surfed the idiot box – apart from nonstop anime and commercial breaks spaced mere seconds apart – I came across countless shows featuring old men in glittery feathery costumes, many of whom were singing and joyfully playing kazoos. Had I had any inkling about Spanish culture other than flamenco at the time, I would have recognised the exuberant frivolity as belonging to the annual Carnaval de Cádiz: a time-honoured festival that has been rollicking on since the 17th century thanks to some good old-fashioned envy.

Back in the day, the city of Cádiz (not to be confused with the *province* of Cádiz, of which the *city* of Cádiz is the capital) was a major seafaring port, just like Venice. After too many years of hearing how amazeballs the masquerade-themed Venice Carnival was from passing ship merchants, the residents of Cádiz (the city, not the province) decided to stage their very own festival.

It helped tremendously that Cádiz was regarded as the comedy capital of Spain – by whom I had no idea – but the sparkly coastal township apparently boasted the highest concentration of wit, humour and sarcasm per capita than anywhere in the country. The unique combination of the Cádizians' *guasa*, or rip-roaring sense of humour, along with their exposure to Colombian, Creole and African music via centuries of merchant trade quickly cemented the Carnaval de Cádiz as one of Europe's most original and best festivals – a tradition that has continued to the present day (much to the chagrin of Venice, I imagine).

With Cádiz spending at least six months preparing for its annual festivities – and most likely another six months cleaning up afterwards – it could well have been that in my nightly jaunts around town, I'd been witnessing rehearsals for the upcoming festival. Seville and Cádiz were only a couple of hours away from each other after all.

From what I could ascertain, the predominant feature of the carnival was choirs, choirs and, astoundingly, more choirs but instead of chanting "Kumbaya", each choral group wrote and performed original satirical ditties that took the piss out of local authority figures and the like. Depending on the fetish of your funny bone, there were four different categories to choose from.

If you considered yourself a bit of an improvising clown with poor time-management and numerical skills, a *cuarteto* was definitely the one for you. Forget the idea of limiting numbers to just four, *cuartetos* ranged in size from three to five performers. As long as you were adept at playing a whistle, clapping stick or kazoo, you were in. The best bit was you could just throw a *cuarteto* together at the last minute and still perform at the festival (so long as you were prepared to be mocked as being *ilegal* by the entire city for not having bothered to officially register on time).

For the more discerning singer who liked their humour tainted with current affairs and wouldn't be caught dead crooning on a street corner, I would recommend joining a *coro*, or large chorus, that belted out tunes of both a funny and serious nature at the top of their lungs whilst being trucked around town on *carruseles*, or flat-bed trailers. Retiring wallflowers, *coros* were not.

If the thought of cracking a smile made your lips chafe, a group of *comparsas* were waiting for you. Accompanied by an extensive backing band, you and your bandmates could be more serious and sing intelligent poetic musings about politics. What's more, you'd never have to fret about what to wear as both you and the 13 or so other male choristers would dress identically.

But really, if you were going to be part of a two-week festival that transformed Cádiz into one giant street party complete with costumed parades and fireworks, you couldn't go past the eccentric *chirigotas*: groups of up to 30 men (with the odd woman thrown into the mix) who wore outlandish matching costumes and sang riotous parodies all over the city. It was those cheery jokers that were hamming it up on a television rerun, vying to be crowned best group. Had I known that the upcoming Carnaval de Cádiz was only days away from kicking off, I would have been there with bells on and little else.

According to Sebastian, if you skipped any class during the week (apart from technique on Tuesdays or Thursdays), Wednesday was the one to miss – the conjecture being that Manuel spent most of the lesson discussing the theory, feel and structure behind each particular *palo*.

'I just want to dance, not talk about it!' Sebastian would protest. My feet, however, were more than happy to have a couple of hours off and I eagerly attended the first session of the day until I remembered that I didn't understand a word of Spanish. Sebastian's boycott was short-lived, for whatever reason, when he turned up to the second class and was duly rewarded by being made to dance a duet with his hot "F@#% You Valentine's Day!" friend Calvin. Had they frocked up and added the tin whistle, they would have been a shoo-in for Carnaval.

In anticipation of Isabel's first lesson back for the week, her class of devoted female followers had tripled in size. She was so popular, her workshops at the neighbouring Festival de Jerez sold out so quickly every year, she often taught two classes *per day* just to accommodate demand. Though I had no clue as to her dancing style, teaching methods or even what she looked like, I knew I was lucky to learn from such a well-loved *maestra* in her hometown.

Right on cue, the pint-sized pocket rocket known as Isabel breezed into the studio smiling, greeting her regulars and welcoming newcomers into the fold with equal affection.

Wearing a belly chain and with a Snoop Dogg sticker plastered on her stereo, the hoop-earringed, raven-haired *guapa* was such the epitome of hip-hop cool, my fashion-forward haircut felt almost acceptable in her presence.

It took the entire class about half an hour to nail (pun intended) the timing for the opening steps of her *rondeña*. All throughout, Isabel was as funny as she was lovely and encouraged us to listen and *otra vez*, try again and again. Even though the studio floor began to feel harder than diamond-reinforced concrete, the students and I were more than happy to drop to the challenge.

Ultimately, there was no point going to multiple flamenco classes (or at least enrolling in them) if you didn't also grasp what you were learning, hence why it was commonplace for students to hire rehearsal rooms after class. Fluffing around in my hotel room day after day wasn't going to cut it (although it did cut the linoleum a bit) so, against Sebastian's fiscal advice of never forking out €5 to hire a studio, I shelled out exactly that to rent one of Manuel's rehearsal rooms.

Upon arrival, I quickly discovered the studio's acoustics were as edgy as my nerves. The moment my shoes hit the floor, every move ricocheted around the room like gunfire and I prayed Manuel was too busy elsewhere to hear me butchering his beloved steps. If only the old wooden floorboards could have imbued me with the secrets of the professional dancers before me but, unfortunately, there was only one way to get better. I ardently hoped some kind of *práctica* would at least make a little *perfección*.

Having always been what you would call an overly enthusiastic teetotaller when it came to metabolising alcohol of any kind, I was pleasantly surprised to discover that in Spain, unlike in Australia, drinking was not a national sport. It wasn't even a hobby. It was just a regular social outlet people enjoyed alongside family, friends, colleagues and pets *without anyone having to get drunk*. You read that correctly. In Spain, and most likely across the entire European continent, alcohol was not primarily consumed to get blotto, wasted, tanked, legless or off your tits, even with a bar on almost every corner.

In Australia, if you were caught anywhere other than a licensed establishment with an open bottle of alcohol, you could expect to receive a delightfully obtuse fine. In Spain, however, public drinking was abundantly encouraged. Mid-afternoon in sunny plazas across the nation, it was not uncommon for a crowd of office workers to share a laugh, *patatas fritas* and several small beers together – a wonderfully inclusive practice known as *botellón*; with the lively atmosphere being the only intoxication. If you couldn't afford drinks from any of the nearby licensed venues, *¡no te preocupes!* You could BYO your own bottle of booze to swig alongside the rest of the townsfolk.

Of course, not everyone could hold their liquor and drunk drivers still abounded but with the way Spaniards drove, there was no real way of telling who was on the sauce or not. At one stage, the federal government considered changing the legal blood alcohol limit from 0.05 to zero tolerance but, like many insanely optimistic ideas, it never took hold. Eighteen was the legal drinking age in Spain, unless you were lucky enough to live in the northern province of Asturias where you could legally get plastered from the tender age of 16. Things were even more interesting up there. At the time of writing, Spain was the only country in the EU that had the lowest age of sexual consent, thanks to the audacious Asturias where, at the ripe old age of 13 – ¡yes 13! – you could legally get your kit off; the only downside being that you had to be sober to do so.

10

EL COSTO DE LAS COSAS
Blowing the Budget

I'd clearly done my research before I'd arrived. Not only was there a supermarket, internet café, additional flamenco school and Sevici bike station within shouting distance of my hotel, but diagonally across the road was an infamous flamenco bar that I had gone all the way into town to enquire about. Thanks to its double-glazed windows, I had been oblivious to the venue's whereabouts but it had explained why most mornings around 3:30 a.m., partygoers suddenly appeared on the streets below my window to continue their rambunctious revelry.

In honour of making it to the end of my first official week in Spain intact – and to counteract the drunken caterwauling I'd been forced to listen to since dawn – I decided to sleep in and skip both of Manuel's technique classes. Not only would it improve my memory retention for the rest of the week, but it would cause me to hyperventilate when I realised that what Manuel taught on Tuesdays and Thursdays was a breakdown of difficult new steps for the following day. If you missed either technique class, you were cactus.

To be fair, I was cactus anyway. With the whirlwind of a foreign city, language, new teachers, lifestyle and unique ways to be kept awake each night, I was feeling pretty left of centre. Unfortunately, there was only one remedy – one singular quest guaranteed to remind me of home whilst simultaneously slapping some sharp perspective into me – and that was to take refuge in the sprawling, homogenous, overly illuminated artificial bubble of a department store.

I've always found retail shopping the most arduous torture ever invented. How anyone could ever enjoy such a stressful pursuit, to the point of finding it therapeutic, was utterly beyond me. A good friend once told me if I had any money to spend in the first place, I might actually enjoy the experience, but I was never convinced. Whenever I absolutely had to purchase something, I would power-walk through shopping malls at the speed of light, hurtling grannies and prams out of my way. If I hadn't found what I wanted within the hour, it was never meant to be. I had a boyfriend once (I've had them other times as well) whose idea of a relaxing weekend was dragging me around men's clothing stores whilst he tried on everything in sight. Needless to say, we didn't last very long.

The irony of seeking out the very pastime that infuriated me back home in order to feel soothed overseas *was* rather amusing but, once safely cocooned within the international interiors of a boundless behemoth, I could be certain of two things: there would be a complimentary working toilet only metres away and I wouldn't have to clutch my belongings as if my life depended on it.

I'd only been learning flamenco for a few weeks when I embarked on the Trafalgar tour of Europe. When our coach arrived in Spain, I was eager to pay a visit to an exclusive flamenco store to try on all of its shoes, accessories and flouncy skirts.* But, as luck would have it, the only days the tour bus visited Madrid and Barcelona – where the stores were located – were on Sundays or public holidays, which meant everything of polka-dotted interest was closed. Whilst my fellow tour passengers were enjoying the local sights, I was sobbing with my nose pressed up against shop windows. The only major outlet that remained open in Barcelona at the time was El Corte Inglés, or The English Cut (as in a tailored cut): Spain's largest and most prominent department store chain. Back then, Ricky Martin's face was plastered on billboards all over the country advertising the place – ensuring it had my instant respect and patronage.

The only Spanish/flamenco word I knew at the time – apart from *olé* – was *zapatos* and, once I found my way to the store's impressive women's shoe department, I was thrilled to find a selection of flamenco shoes for sale. I didn't give a toss that they were beginner's styles because they were authentic and they were from Spain. A pair of black leather size 37s proved the perfect fit and, thanks to a smattering of nail tips underneath, they ended up making

---

* Disclaimer: flamenco accessories are only one of two exceptions I will admit to enjoying shopping for; the other is food.

a hell of a lot more noise than the character shoes I'd been wearing in class.

The only downside to my coveted new purchase was, after having worn them in, the shoes began to stink so pungently, fumigators had to be called in whenever I took them off. After four years of faithful service, they were retired to the back of my wardrobe where they've been doing a wonderful job of keeping moths out ever since.

That was the thing about flamenco. When you were just starting out, fellow dancers were too busy maxing out their credit cards to warn you that you were about to become addicted to one of the most expensive hobbies in the world. Shoes aside, unless you were a whiz on the sewing machine, you either had to pay to get a flamenco dress custom-made or risk buying one online (after which time you'd most likely still have to pay to get it altered.)

Having fluffed around in flamenco classes for several years, I was honoured to be invited to fluff around in my teacher's exclusive dance troupe and spent the next few years pinching myself as my fellow ensemble dancers and I performed at countless theatres, festivals and events up and down the east coast of Australia. Spotty material was a rare commodity at the time and when my friends and I weren't rehearsing, attending classes or travelling to and from shows, we were obsessed with finding fabric.

Once we'd eventually secured enough material for a family of 10 to fashion a tent out of, we each then had to find a dressmaker brave enough to take on the Herculean challenge. In the beginning, seamstresses charged us exorbitant fees to concoct frilly creations from kilometres of material, before they refused to ever work for us again. (My first red dress cost $440 AUD alone, material not included.)

Several years later, when in New York with my mother, I was delighted to find an outlet for the very same flamenco store that I'd missed out on in Spain. Without hesitation, I went completely and spectacularly *loca* and blew $1,000 in just 20 minutes. (That was before my back gave out and my mother had to carry our bags around town.) Had I paid too much? Due to the exchange rate, most likely. But to this day, my red suede shoes, red-and-white polka-dotted skirt with so many frills it could take a man's eye out, colourful roses and pair of spotty earrings remain one of THE most satisfying purchases of my life. Perhaps my friend was right about shopping being *slightly* enjoyable after all.

Back in Seville, I fell all too quickly into the familiar embrace of the city's central El Corte Inglés store and, rather than heading straight to its shoe section, my stomach and I made a beeline for the grocery department instead. Bright sparkly fridges enticed me over to their colourful wares of *chorizo*, wine, cheese, chocolate and gourmet delights. I would have happily spent the next few hours salivating over *salmón y sorbetes* if a certain sign hadn't caught my eye.

'*SIN GLUTEN*' the placard announced.

My blood sugar and I were too fragile to be trifled with

but, sure enough, in a cheery display all on its own was the most extensively glorious selection of gluten-free pastry products I had EVER seen. Pizza bases, baguettes, muffins, brioches, chocolate wafers and sweet biscuits; every single one of them was *sin gluten*. It was all I could do to remain conscious.

Without a moment's hesitation, I started grabbing packets of hamburger buns and savoury biscuits and stuffed as many into the crook of my arm as I could carry. That was, until I came across the croissants – a luscious luxury my sensitive stomach hadn't allowed me to taste in over a decade. Could you imagine what that did to a person?! Try walking past a bakery smelling the wafting aromas of freshly baked bread knowing you'd get sick if you ate any of it. No wonder I was so cranky all the time. A packet of gluten-free, chocolate-filled croissants completed the indulgent lineup. Rain, hail or shine, I was going on a pastry bender.

'*Do you want to meet up somewhere this arvo?*' It was a text from Sebastian.

'*¡Sí, por favor!*' I instantly replied.

Spending the afternoon reminiscing with my dear friend would be the ideal way to quash any remaining bouts of homesickness. I smiled as I envisioned us indulging in every kind of potato dish available at some funky *tapas* bar, washed down with a couple of glasses of fresh, fruity *sangría*. The reality was *un poquito diferente*: Sebastian and I sat on the banks of the Guadalquivir and shared my only bottle of water. Regardless of the fact that I had used up every last drop of savings to get to Spain, and was living on a budget tighter than a hippo in spandex, the infamous adage still applied: *mi casa es tu casa*. There was no way I would be telling Sebastian about any of my newly purchased pastry products though.

I looked out across the calm waters of the river and took a deep breath. It was time to broach a subject that had been on my mind for days.

'Hey, Seb,' I began with *trepidación*.

'Yeah, Stace?'

'Um ... do you know where the coin-operated laundries are?'

I had only a couple more days of undies to see me through and I wasn't too keen on splurging on the excessive dry cleaning fees at the hotel. Ever the *optimista*, Sebastian declared laundry facilities cost too much money and that I should just handwash everything I owned. Had he not taken inventory of how many layers I'd been wearing? Did he not realise the sheer strength involved in wringing out wet winter clothes?! One jumper alone could severely impact a girl's ability to do *floreos*, or wrist flourishes, in class.

To be honest, I didn't have the best track record with international laundries. In downtown San Francisco once (on our way back from New York), my mother and I spent hours walking up and down treacherous hills lugging heavy bags of dirty clothing until we found a laundry that was open. Not wanting to cart around a weighty bottle of washing liquid as well, we figured we would just pay for detergent once we got there.

The laundry's vending machine offered a fairly basic range of liquid cleaners, all of which I shunned in favour of some ahead of the curve, cheap new tissue-looking detergent technology. It wasn't until our clothes were being spun-dry that I read the fine print on the back of the packet and discovered that the wondrous piece of material was just a flimsy tissue that acted like some kind of inept buffer. With no more loose change in our pockets, my mother stood guard over our still-dirty clothes, while I raced up yet another hill to find a convenience store, where I bought some actual detergent and asked for change to get more @#%$ quarters so we could start the whole process again. Actually, when you counted up the mental and physical cost of an afternoon spent screaming at hills, check-out chicks, washing machines and family members, dry cleaning didn't seem so bad.

Having encountered so much trouble laundering my clothes in an English-speaking country, I conceded Sebastian had a valid point and, over the following days, I dutifully handwashed my body weight in winter clothing in the hotel's bathtub. Trying to decipher which was laundry detergent and which was dishwashing liquid in the local supermarket simply added to the *experiencia*.

When a dancer friend of mine first visited Seville's Casa de la Memoria, she became so platonically besotted with a performer by the name of Maribel that she ended up bringing her all the way out to Brisbane to teach a workshop, during which Maribel taught the most kick-arse *alegría con mantón* you could ever imagine – a happy dance made even more jovial because it involved flinging a shawl around.

Having never owned a *mantón*, or large shawl, myself I'd asked a skyscraper of a student if I could borrow one of hers for the weekend. Her colourful creation was so impressively hefty, it could have doubled as a sail on a yacht and I spent most of the workshop trying not to step on its tassels or take anyone's eye out. Had the students and I ended up performing the dance at our end-of-year concert, not only would our shawls have become deeply entangled with one another's but, most likely, with members of the audience and the lighting rig as well.

When I read that the very same Maribel was to perform at the Casa de la Memoria, I couldn't miss the chance to see her and managed to secure one of the last seats in the second row. For the first number, the band – made up of a Latino-looking Meat Loaf on guitar, and Ben Lee's Spanish-looking cousin on vocals – played a rhythmic *tango* to get everyone in the mood. Then, when Maribel appeared she was just as I remembered: gorgeous and diminutive, with long, lustrous eyelashes and looks that would give Nigella Lawson a run for her money. With her hair swept up in a 1920s style, she was the epitome of elegance and grace – that was, until she unleashed the beast.

For the first dance, Maribel threw herself body and soul into an intensely dramatic *soleá*. Her upper body was rapid-fire, elastic and agitated; her legs so heavy and powerful, it was as if they were being pulled down into the depths of the earth. Such was the grip of her *pasión formidable* and unapologetic agony, she became almost unrecognisable and glared fiercely and directly into the soul of her audience – demanding that we joined her on her journey of despair, throughout which she knocked the stuffing out of us with her blistering assault.

As a kind of sobering sorbet to cleanse the emotional palate, Spanish Meat Loaf played a melancholic *taranta* on guitar. The audience soon became lost in reflective reverie until Maribel emerged once more, whether we were ready for her or not. She shifted gears entirely and lightened the mood with a flawless *alegría*, complimented beautifully by a smoking hot, red-and-cream pant suit, matching jacket and shiny cream-coloured shoes (just no shawl). For the finale, a mystery male dancer materialised out of nowhere and joined her for a *bulería*, but all eyes remained firmly planted on the evocative Maribel.

All eyes and a camera, that was. Every night before the show commenced, audiences were expressly told in three different languages that filming of any kind was not permitted. Only still photographs were allowed and only during *el final*. A middle-aged man directly in front of me obviously felt that the rules did not apply to him and proceeded to film the entire closing number. After the show, I informed the female emcee. Without blinking an eyelid, she replied, 'Oh, he must be French.' It was *una posibilidad*, I guessed.

When Maribel surfaced from the dressing room afterwards, gone was the fiery flamenco deity and in her place was the soft, lovely, funny lady I remembered from Brisbane. Only after I introduced myself, I remembered she spoke even less English than I knew Spanish, but she was such a trooper throughout our clumsy *conversación*, she generously offered for me to contact her if I needed anything while I was in Seville. At least that's what I think she said.

The squeaky strains of "'O Sole Mio" courtesy of a busker with a badly tuned violin accompanied my sojourn back through the cobblestoned courtyards of Seville until an unexpected sight commanded my attention. Six young women were posing for photographs in front of the old cathedral – which was certainly harmless enough – were it not for the fact that each one of them was also bent over, mooning the photographer. If ever there was the quintessential moment to shout '*¡Arsa!*' in Andalucía that had to be it.

11

PERDIDO EN LA TRADUCCIÓN
Lost in Translation

The best part about flamenco workshops was, apart from getting up close and personal with good-looking instructors, you could be taught almost an entire dance in just a few short days. Learning the exact same sequence in class, however, could take several months once you factored in the development of crucial technique and a deeper understanding of the rhythmic *compás*. It was no wonder then that dropping in for a fortnight of intensive dance lessons, whilst attempting to master complex choreography that had been in the making for over six months, would be enough to test anyone's *paciencia*.

At Manuel's studio, I watched with increasing anxiety as he divided the students into *grupos* to perform the dance from the very beginning. Usually, I stood on the sidelines until I recognised some of the newer steps, but for some reason Manuel encouraged me to join in and emulate not only the choreography but the *muy importante* style and feel as well.

When he clapped his hands together and shouted, '*¡Y!*' it was *de vida o muerte* (do or die). I scurried to the back of the room and tried in vain to mimic the students in front, but nothing could hide my fear nor flailing limbs. Shortly thereafter, Manuel and I mutually agreed for me to go back to Plan A: complete and utter abstinence.

The mental and physical fatigue continued to take its toll over at Isabel's. Whenever I repeated a step back to her, the *confusión* on her face spoke volumes as if we were speaking entirely different choreographic languages. No matter how hard I tried to emulate her style, my approach seemed to resemble nothing she had ever seen before, nor seemingly wanted to see again. Whilst I personally considered that to be a real skill, it did nothing for my dwindling confidence.

As I skulked back to the hotel, I was astounded to compute that I had just danced 14 hours in the past five days. The only thing keeping me upright was a devout loyalty to a secret ritual whispered throughout the hallowed halls of flamenco studios since time immemorial, and that was – regardless of the temperature outside – to soak your aching feet in a bucket filled with the most freezing, iciest subzero water available until they, and the rest of your body, went numb with shock. Frosty footbaths were literally the sole reason (pun intended) that I could still walk after class each day.

With *Esposas Desperadas* (the dubbed Spanish version of *Desperate Housewives*) on in the background, I filled the noodle cooking pot with cold tap water, threw in a plethora of ice cubes and soaked my throbbing feet. As I tucked into some gluten-free crackers sandwiched around *chorizo*, it suddenly dawned on me what an enormous voiceover industry there must have been dubbing imported foreign shows into Spanish. Why on earth didn't they just use subtitles?!

Two words: General Franco. When the dictatorial despot first came to power, he decreed his country contained far too many vernaculars so, to make things easier (no doubt for him), he anointed Castilian as the official native tongue and, throughout his reign, ordered all foreign content to be dubbed exclusively in that language.

But as is wont to happen under the iron-fisted rule of an oppressive tyrant meddling with mass media, the lines between translation and censorship soon became blurred as characters and dialogue were completely rewritten to promote Franco's totalitarian vision – which was not without its complications. If a television show depicted an unmarried couple unchastely living together in sin, their relationship was instantly changed to that of brother and sister; but before anyone could yell, *¡Incesto!* all physical contact between said "siblings" was also edited out. If anyone's "sister" got pregnant, I assumed the rest of the series was then shelved.

Hundreds of productions were sanitised that way up until Franco's death in 1975 but by then, the Spanish voiceover industry had become so firmly entrenched, dubbing continued to be the preferred form of translation, which was great news if you aspired to be an *actor de doblaje*, or professional dubbing actor.

If you were good, you could be chosen to be the Spanish voice of a Hollywood movie star for the entire length of their career. If you were *really* good, you could be allocated multiple celebrities. Imagine coming up with different character voices for Bruce Willis, Willem Dafoe and Kevin Costner? Some guy did. How about Darth Vader, the Terminator and Clint Eastwood? The only challenge would be remembering whose voice belonged to whom, especially if all three happened to be in the same scene at the same time.

One of the most famous Spanish dubbing actors of all time was Carlos Revilla – a former medical student-turned-prolific voiceover artist – who voiced Alan Alda, Groucho Marx, Michael Caine, Cary Grant and Kitt from Knight Rider to name but a few. But Carlos' biggest claim to fame was as the Spanish voice of Homer Simpson (a separate actor dubbed the Latin American version of *Los Simpson*). Sadly, Carlos passed away in 2000 but was swiftly replaced by another man (also named Carlos), who added James Gandolfini from *The Sopranos* and Dean Norris from *Breaking Bad* to his repertoire. But since Gandolfini's death and the dearth of *Breaking Bad*, the new Carlos has had a bit more time on his hands.

The best gig in the industry, though, would have to belong to the people who dreamt up Spanish versions of English film and television titles. Regardless of whether a production used voiceovers or subtitles, it still needed an Hispanic name and that was where poetic license could run delightfully rampant.

Interpretations could be literal or liberal. Jim Carrey's *The Cable Guy* was changed to *Un Loco a Domicilio* or "A Madman in the House". Classic series *Knight Rider* was known as *El Auto Fantástico* ("The Fantastic Car"), which hopefully wasn't too confusing when *Cuatro Fantásticos* ("The

Fantastic Four") was released. *Ferris Bueller's Day Off* was renamed as *Todo En Un Día* or "All in One Day" which, I suppose, was technically correct; as was *Weekend at Bernie's* which was changed to – spoiler alert – *Este Muerto Está Muy Vivo* or "This Dead Person is Very Much Alive".

However, if there was ever a Lifetime Achievement Award given out for the Most Irrelevant Spanish Language Film Title Translation, it would have to be a toss-up between *Sonrisas y Lágrimas*, aka "Smiles and Tears" (a baffling name for *The Sound of Music*), or the macho flick *Die Hard* – which was renamed *Jungla de Cristal* or "The Glass Jungle" (which, I assume, referred to modern skyscrapers, in which case any movie set in a freaking city would qualify).

As my feet turned into stumpy blue iceblocks, any confounding confusion I felt over such nationalistic anomalies proved only temporary as I had an increasing case of heartburn to contend with, forcing me to conclude that one *could,* in fact, consume too much *chorizo* in one sitting. The tenants above attempted to distract me by playing chess with their furniture, before repeatedly opening and shutting their dresser drawers for the remainder of the evening. Their kind gesture, combined with the usual drunken revelry from the bar across the road, random hammering and a truck unloading beneath my window at 4 a.m. ensured any *indigestión* was swiftly replaced with *insomnio*.

Gracias.

12

LAS SEVILLANAS
The Never-ending Songs

Some flamenco student I was. I had been in Spain for over a week and hadn't even bought so much as a castanet. With a whole day off, I was finally ready to splurge on any and all manner of flamenco accessories; it was just a pity that by the time I hit the streets, everything was closed for *siesta*.

As a nana-napping night owl from way back, I adored the idea of a cultural catnap and dearly wished it would be implemented worldwide – allowing everybody to sleep in, start work mid-morning, linger over lunch, pass out for a couple of hours, go back to work and then head out for a late dinner. In short: enjoying life. But not everyone was in favour of having forty winks. Some naysaying stick-in-the-muds from the Spanish Parliamentary Commission once put forward a ridiculous motion to abolish the *siesta* and replace it with a 9-to-5 workday, with the pretense of lifting Spain out of its economic crisis. Surely forcing an entire population to change harmonious habits they'd been observing for *generaciones* would make them miserable – not to mention the detrimental impact it would have on flamenco if everyone was tucked up in bed by 10 p.m. each night.

It was probably just as well the shops were closed as I was supposed to be spending the day sightseeing with Sebastian. He had messaged the previous evening saying he was looking forward to having an early night in the share house he'd just moved into and would see me in the morning.

At 2 p.m. a bleary-eyed, softly spoken Sebastian turned up at my door. As he munched his way through my garlic potato chips, all he could remember from the previous night's shenanigans was eating *churros* on his own somewhere on the side of the road in Triana at 6 a.m. It sounded like a riveting evening.

Sebastian then invited me over to check out his new pad, which happened to only be a few blocks away from my hotel. 'Do you mind if I borrow one of your towels?' he requested. 'I haven't had a shower yet.'

'You don't have any at your new place?'

'Nah, I haven't had time to buy any yet.'

Lucky for him, I had one clean towel remaining that had not been involved in either drying my body, frozen feet or handwashing. Sebastian's flatmates weren't able to loan him one of theirs as they'd already taken off to Cádiz, presumably with all of their linen. The only thing his flatmates *had* managed to leave behind though, apart from the living quarters in a complete shemozzle, was remnants of *cocaína* on the communal coffee table.

Once Sebastian cleaned himself and his apartment up a little, he invited me to join him at a percussion party later that evening. The last thing I wanted to do was to miss out on another social occasion, so I happily accepted both the invitation and my used towel back, before I raced back to the hotel to get ready. With a little bit of time before we were to meet up with Sebastian's friends, I returned to his place to hang out. Predictably, there was only one thing on his mind.

'Ah ha ha ha ha ha! Look at their faces!' Sebastian roared with laughter as we watched online videos of his all-time favourite practical jokes being played on people. Every time some poor unsuspecting soul awoke with a fright from a brass band striking up in their bedroom or had the living daylights scared out of them by someone screaming at them from around a corner, Sebastian fell into hysterics.

'Comedy gold, Stace,' he would declare, wiping his eyes.

Ding.

A text message appeared on his phone. The rendezvous was on.

A sassy, blonde bombshell of a woman named Paloma squealed with delight when she spotted Sebastian and me at the bar and gave us both a warm, vivacious welcome. By her side was Ricardo, a former waiter-turned-professional flamenco guitarist, whom I assumed was also her date for the evening.

As Sebastian and his friends conversed animatedly in the local lingo, I decided to keep the Spanish economy afloat by knocking back glasses of *vino tinto* and platefuls of *carne y patatas fritas*. It was just after midnight when Paloma received the long-awaited text.

'*Vámonos!*' she declared and hastened us for a quick departure.

'Ricardo's not joining us?' I asked Sebastian as we exited the bar.

'Nah, he's a guitarist. Percussion parties aren't his thing.' Neither, it seemed, was Paloma.

Space-saving ingenuity was on full display on the streets outside where cars were literally parked on footpaths and curbs at every intersection. Bumper bars were so tantalisingly close, they were practically touching. The only way drivers could manoeuvre their vehicles in or out of parking spots appeared to be to ricochet off everyone else's vehicle. If you were an out-of-work panel beater, I would highly recommend the place.

Before you could say, 'Does this thing have seatbelts?' with a screech of tyres we were off and careening through the streets of Seville in Paloma's clapped out *limón* of a car in which speed limits, giving way and applying the brakes were entirely optional. With all of the windows down (most likely because they were broken), Paloma's long, golden locks flickered in the wind like Medusa's, whilst in the backseat I found myself unwittingly transported back to my youth by playing "Corners" as I was dramatically flung from side to side every time the car turned. No wonder Sebastian sat in the front.

A short time later, we pulled up at a ramshackle neighbourhood where, defying his dilapidated surroundings, a striking *gitano* in an immaculate green suit stood waiting for us; his long, raven hair shimmering in the moonlight like it was auditioning for a Pantene commercial. Not only was he arrestingly attractive, but Señor Stunning was the guest of honour for the percussion party – in that he was the percussionist. After brief introductions were made, Sebastian joined me in the backseat to play "Corners", whilst Spanish Fabio, his luscious locks and *cajón* rode shotgun with Paloma.

'What is this place?' I whispered to Sebastian when, minutes later, we screeched to a halt in front of a rundown, wooden-looking shack.

'You'll see.' He winked.

To say the bar was a blast from the past was an understatement. In amongst the crowded throng were tatty cane chairs, mismatched couches and beer barrels. Above, a giant television – powered by electrical leads that dangled tantalisingly from the rafters – campaigned for wall space alongside an obligatory bull's head and smattering of bullfighting memorabilia. The resident band, all of whom were wearing Converse shoes (it must have been a flamenco thing) were rocking out in the far corner.

Paloma, Fabio, Sebastian and I squeezed our way through to the bar where a couple of their friends were waiting: Abigail, a chic, auburn-haired fashionista from France and the infamous "F@#% You Valentine's Day!" instigator himself – Calvin.

'*Vino?*' Calvin shouted over the din.

'*Sí!*' I yelled. '*Tinto, por favor!*'

Really, it didn't matter what anyone's drink of choice was as all liquids either ended up spilled on the blackened tile floor, or all over everyone else as bar patrons attempted to balance their glasses and clap along in time to the music. After *muchos vinos*, I couldn't help but notice a heightened boisterous energy suddenly pervade the room. The crowd's shouts of *jaleos* became louder and more insistent until their unanimous demands gained so much momentum, they could no longer be ignored. The hordes were baying for one thing and one thing only: the unofficial anthem of their city known as *las sevillanas*.

No social gathering of more than one person is considered complete in Seville without attempting to sing or perform the city's internationally notorious alternative to "The Nutbush". What started out as an old-school folk dance in the 18th century has evolved into a classic party tune of such unceasing repetition, there are no plans for it to disappear up the wazoo anytime soon. The fact that the *sevillanas* is not considered true flamenco amongst purists has done nothing to dim its popularity amongst the masses. It is the partnered dance of the people, so wildly loved that at any given time, some Spaniards somewhere will be dancing it (including outside hotel windows at 3 a.m.).

Every year, the whole town goes s*evillanas* crazy at the annual *Feria* festival, where everyone from babies to grannies deck themselves out in bright, garish *sevillana* costumes and dance up a storm. By day, you can marvel at horse processions whilst you gorge yourself on overpriced seafood, before you risk your life on a shoddily built carnival ride in the aptly named Calle del Infierno, or Hell Street. By night, beautiful lantern displays illuminate everyone's polka dots as partygoers drink themselves silly on sherry and dance *sevillanas* until they drop. (No doubt you can do the latter in the daytime, too.) If you hadn't known how to dance *sevillanas* before the festival, you could pretty much teach it by the end.

To the outsider, each *sevillana* looks like the same dance repeated ad nauseam: couples spin around on the spot, and each other, as their arms flail about like windmills – which isn't too far off the mark. The traditional version comprises four short songs of roughly one minute each, all of which *sound* almost identical. Each *sevillana* has its own unique choreography that features turns, rotating limbs and fluffing about on the spot, all of which *look* almost identical. The only way you can truly tell them apart is by their imaginative titles: Number One, Two, Three or Four.

It never matters in which order you dance a *sevillana*, the golden rule is just to tell your partner which one you want to do next. If you break into Number Four when he or she has just started Number Two, you had better brace yourselves. However, so long as you both finish with a wrist flourish on the final note (and haven't caused too many life-threatening injuries along the way), all will be forgiven.

Back at the bar, a frenzy erupted when the resident band began playing the opening bars of the first *sevillana* of the evening. Every patron in attendance, regardless of their mobility, senility or sobriety jumped up, grabbed a partner and began dancing with wild abandon. Everyone, it seemed, but me as I stood impatiently on the sidelines watching Calvin and Sebastian take turns to dance with Paloma and Abigail. I should have taken a leaf out of one plucky, and rather tipsy, lady's book. Not having a partner didn't stop her in the slightest. She made up her own solo version, complete with flamboyant turns, wrist trills and brazen flair.

After several rounds of *sevillanas*, Sebastian pulled me onto the dance floor.

'Three?' I asked eagerly over the musical introduction.

'Let's do Two,' Sebastian responded; a wonderful plan, if only I could have remembered how the darned thing went. That was the thing about *sevillanas* – being the least-practised dance of any performance repertoire, it was usually the first to go tits up.

When the crowd's hunger for *sevillanas* was temporarily sated, Fabio was invited onstage to play *cajón* and instantly blew everyone away with his blazingly brilliant talent and captivating beauty. He would've been the perfect man, if only he hadn't spent more time on his hair than me.

The rest of the evening descended into a blur of sherry, *sevillanas* and shouting until, just before 4 a.m., Paloma stormed out of the bar. Not wanting to be abandoned in the boondocks, Sebastian, Calvin and I quickly followed suit and had just enough time to squeeze into her car before she sped off, leaving Fabio and his *cajón* in her blistering wake. As we zipped and ducked through the back streets of Seville, the boys struggled to comfort a very shaken and stirred Paloma. I sensed a love triangle had been brewing.

Before we left the bar, I'd seen Fabio chatting to Abigail, the other dancer from class, and had thought nothing of it. But as it turned out, the Latin lothario had been asking Abigail if he could sleep at her place that night – as in sleep *with* her. There would have been no problem with such a proposition if it weren't for the fact that, for the past fortnight, Fabio had been exclusively dating Paloma and had declared his undying love to her – until he met Abigail. To really stick the flamenco boot in, when Fabio asked Abigail to go home with him, it was *in front* of Paloma.

With Calvin having to be up in a matter of hours to teach English and Paloma in no mood to continue partying, Sebastian and I were dropped off at La Madrugá – the infamous flamenco bar across the road from my hotel. I was chuffed to finally see inside the mythical institution but, unfortunately, it was filled with so much smoke and jam-packed with so many sweaty bodies, I never really saw too much.

'Hold onto my arm, Stace,' Sebastian advised as he did his best battering ram impersonation and pushed us towards the main bar where, over a beer or two, Sebastian proceeded to enlighten me about the romantic reputation of *gitanos*. Non-*gitana* women were like catnip to such charmingly flirty boys who seemingly practised the art of disposable dating by moving from one *guapa* to the next at dizzying speeds. When it inevitably came time to settle down though, *gitano* boys almost always ended up marrying *gitana* girls. I would have loved for some gorgeous, doe-eyed *gitano* to pledge his love to me, even for just a moment but, thanks to my new closely cropped haircut, I'd probably only attract a *gitana* or two.

13

DESVIACIONES DEL DESCUBRIMIENTO
The Accidental Tourist

According to a flamenco brochure I'd acquired at the central tourist office, smack bang in the middle of Seville was a three-level museum devoted entirely to the art of flamenco dance.

¿¿Disculpe?!

¡¿A flamenco dance museum?!

When I checked the opening times, my heart soared with joy. It was actually open, and on a Sunday of all days! What's more, there would be ample time to explore the exhibits before Sebastian took me sightseeing for the afternoon.

What a tremendously satisfying morning it was. The museum's displays were as beguiling as they were beautiful; designed to invoke as much overwhelming passion from viewers as possible. The fervour from souls past and present was palpable throughout the exhibit's endlessly compelling and carefully curated videos and interviews. Stirring, surround-sound melodies laden with grief and sorrow emptied my heart and brought me to tears, before racks of exquisitely ornate flamenco dresses revived me back to life.

Even the museum's restrooms were a work of art, imbued with soft, warm tones and a smattering of rose petals throughout. I was so mesmerised by the rust-coloured walls, free-standing ceramic basins and lush floral decorations, I walked straight into the bathroom's full-length mirror, believing it to be an adjoining room of the ladies' loo. The fact that a slightly recognisable, weary-looking, punk-haired traveller was walking towards me failed to register at the time.

The dizziness persevered in the museum's gift shop, where I unquestionably handed over €5 for a pair of "professional standard" *castañuelas* (castanets) that turned out to be so dodgy, they ended up keeping my stinky flamenco shoes company in the back of my wardrobe. That was what I called an investment.

As I wandered back through Triana, a familiar figure headed towards me – and for once it wasn't my reflection.

'Seb?' I called out.

'Oh hey, Stace.' Sebastian pedalled over on what I assumed was one of his flatmate's bicycles.

'Where are you off to?' I asked in a puzzled tone.

'Back to my place. I'm helping a friend design his website.'

'Oh, I see.' My eyes darted to the Burger King bag dangling from the handlebars.

'Sorry, Stace, I better get back to my friend, but see you in class tomorrow?' He turned to leave.

'Um sure.' I nodded and watched him pedal away.

Really, who needed a knowledgeable local tour guide for the afternoon anyway? I would do just as well on my own, thank you very much. To hell with the local haunts and hard to find places, my inner tourist and I were going to go all out and visit one of the biggest attractions in town: the Plaza de España.

Why it was called the Square of Spain I would never fathom as it was much more curvaceous than quadrilateral, with a huge sandstone-coloured building wrapped around an enormous semi-circular courtyard. But when it was such an impressive expanse of architecture, who really cared what it was called? The best features were the moats which, along with the central Vicente Traver fountain, would have been vastly more impressive had they actually contained any water.

Four ornate bridges that just happened to represent the four ancient kingdoms of Spain (Castile, León, Aragon and Navarre, in case you were wondering) provided a pretty passage across the barren waterways. At the base of the main building were the Alcoves of the Provinces – painted tiled mosaics, or *azulejos*, that depicted each of the 48 Spanish provinces. Unfortunately, most of these beautiful creations were cordoned off for maintenance so the closest anyone could get was taking a photograph of a photograph plastered on the barriers out the front.

Like me, the Plaza de España has led a colourful life. Originally built to house an international expo in 1929, the area proved to be such a unique location that, 30 years later, Hollywood came calling in the guise of *Lawrence of Arabia*; the production of which transformed the site into an Egyptian hotel. More recently, the plaza featured in one of the newer *Star Wars* movies but, luckily, they found it in their budget to get the fountains working. Normally, boring old government offices is all you'd find in the plaza's *grandioso* main building but, come the weekend, tourists could enjoy horse and buggy rides whilst they haggled with vendors over the price of their flimsy shawls.

Over by one of the alcoves, a bunch of sightseers had gathered to watch a flamenco guitarist and his *cantaor* play and sing nonstop *sevillanas*. I was tempted to grab one of the threadbare excuses for a shawl and dance for the enthusiastic crowd but figured my appearance fee wasn't worth the effort and besides, I would have been pickpocketed on the way out anyway.

Back in my dark, frosty cave of an apartment, the stale stench of decaying, mouldy handwashing that had taken several days to dry had finally become unbearable. It was only then, after 10 full days of being a resident in the hotel that I miraculously found each one of the window panes in my room contained a built-in horizontal blind that could be manually opened or closed with the twist of a knob. Once I was finally able to see *and* feel the light, not only would my handwashing dry in record time, but I could simultaneously sunbathe in bed with a gluten-free croissant if I so desired.

14

INMORTAL
Some of Us Live Forever

It was like a UN summit in the ladies' changing room at Manuel's. Whether the students hailed from Japan, Brazil, Russia, Taiwan, France or Spain, when it came to removing their sweaty dance clothes in the open-plan changing room, there seemed to be only two ways to go about it. Depending on the level of cultural inhibition, some students hid in the corner and tried to flash the least amount of flesh possible as they jiggled and squirmed about like they were trying to escape from a straitjacket. Others stood brazenly in the middle of the room and chatted away to anyone who would listen with nothing but their knickers on. (No prizes for guessing which camp I belonged to.)

Just as my aching feet and I finished up at Isabel's, Paloma and Abigail arrived for the more advanced class. I was relieved to note I wasn't the only rebel attending two different flamenco schools (an unpardonable sin back in Australia) but, more importantly, that the girls hadn't allowed Spanish Fabio, or his luscious locks, to come between them.

Back at the apartment, I had somehow run out of clean clothes yet again and, after I threw myself into another handwashing frenzy, I took off for my last private rehearsal at Manuel's studio; trying in vain to ignore the fact that €5 could have bought me a glass of wine and a good time at the local laundry instead.

One of my ultimate ambitions (apart from snogging hot Spanish men) has always been to see Paco de Lucía, the greatest flamenco guitarist of all time, live in concert. The brief times the glorious freak of melodious nature ever toured seemed only to be to Europe or the Americas. The closest Australia came to encountering his brilliance was when Paco's brother was invited to play guitar at the Adelaide Festival once. Close, but no *cigarro*.

In the late 1960s, Paco was fatefully introduced to a young singer by the name of Camarón – a Cádiz *gitano* whose incredibly raw, emotive vocals quickly immortalised him as the greatest flamenco singer of all time. The inevitable collaboration of the greatest singer and greatest guitarist resulted in an historic partnership that spanned decades and together, they produced over 10 albums that are still considered masterpieces today. Sadly, Camarón passed away when he was just 42 years old and, even more tragically as

I was writing this book, Paco suffered a fatal heart attack and died at the age of 66, plunging the flamenco world into eternal mourning. The only consolation was, although I never witnessed his incredible genius live in concert, Paco would forever be my friend on MySpace (until I deleted my account).

Before anyone else carked it, I made my way back to the charming Casa de la Memoria to absorb some more flamenco. I'd even booked a ticket beforehand, which was most unlike me but, regardless of whether I had rung up or rocked up, somehow I always ended up in a great spot.

'*Prima!*' I whispered when I found myself seated beside an elderly German couple in the second row. Finally it was my chance to show off my impressive language skills honed through five years of high school German and four days hurtling through their motherland in an air-conditioned tour bus. Visions of the three of us sharing a hearty laugh over *Glühwein* and *tapas* after the performance were quickly dashed, however, when my gaping memory and sloppy pronunciation of their language became all too evident; leading the couple to conclude that I was, in fact, Italian. *Stupendo.*

Once our awkward small talk was out of the way, Mrs Frau pulled out a notebook and began sketching members of the audience. She continued to do so even after the show commenced, causing her to miss most of what was an electrifying evening courtesy of the headline dancer Pastora Galván. Not to worry. In years to come, Mrs Frau could make a flipbook from her drawings as she reminisced about all the ignorant tourists who had slept through one of the most passionate displays of soulful art ever to have graced the planet.

The Spanish equivalent of Spring Break – where teenagers customarily got plastered, pregnant, stoned and arrested in no particular order – was in full swing back at the hotel. Excited, amplified voices and slammed doors ricocheted down the corridors all evening, which made me pine for the furniture movers above. By early morning I was ready to throw myself out of the window but instead, I threw on some jeans and marched down to reception to demand they tell the students to shut-the-#@$%-up. Ever the exemplary example of customer service, the desk clerk informed me that it was their teacher's responsibility and gave me her room number.

Frantic knocks and cranky English soon woke said teacher from what appeared to be her only snippets of sanity. Without missing a beat, the teacher marched down the hall, knocked on every single student's door and put an immediate end to the night of deafening debauchery. I would have then enjoyed a sumptuous slumber myself if I hadn't been so completely wound up.

15

FARALAES
Frilly Frou-frou

'*Eso es.*'

Manuel was observing everyone's footwork throughout the studio. As I contorted my torso into a pretzel and tried to keep my feet moving at a rapid-fire pace, whilst remembering to keep my chest puffed out like a peacock, Manuel directed an '*Eso es*' my way. Much to my relief, rather than declaring an emergency, anything that rhymed with SOS in flamenco was actually an encouragement along the lines of 'That's it!' To celebrate my triumph, I elected to treat myself to a whole new flamenco wardrobe.

The best thing about shopping for flamenco outfits in Andalucía was there was an exhaustive range of *sevillana*-style dresses and skirts to choose from. The worst thing about shopping for flamenco outfits in Andalucía was that there was *only* an exhaustive range of *sevillana*-style dresses and skirts available. Designs had changed dramatically over the years, evolving from voluminous meringues to restrictive, form-fitting cocoons that had become so snug, your ankles never spent more than a few millimetres apart. The fundamental joy of such slinky numbers was, though, no matter how big your bum or muffin top was, once you'd stuffed yourself into the elongated casing of a *sevillana* dress, you would be instantly transformed into a lanky, curvy, gorgeous Latina – just so long as you didn't want to walk, sit down or breathe at the same time.

There was no end to the abundance of designer dresses on sale in the centre of Seville, and no end to their price tags either. Taking a detour off the main drag, I was rewarded with a glorious flamenco store I hadn't previously noticed. It may have looked like all of its contemporaries with numerous shawls, accessories and exquisite dresses on display, but there was something different about it that inextricably caught my attention. As soon as I stepped inside, a kindly older lady greeted me as if I was the one she'd been waiting for all day. I took it as a sign.

'*Yo quiero un vestido de sevillana, por favor.*' I proudly shared my heart's desire with her. Who knew what the shop assistant said in return, but it sounded something like, 'Honey, don't even bother yourself with the display dresses down here. There's a whole floor of costumes upstairs where your wildest dreams are about to come true.'

I dutifully followed the matronly assistant up a narrow, wooden stairwell into what could only be described as flamenco nirvana. Racks and racks of wildly polka-dotted *sevillana* masterpieces filled the entire upper level. Needless to say, within seconds, I went *bananas* and tried on every

Spanish Cinderella costume the shopkeeper gave me. Each garment was stunning and flattering and made me feel like a million bucks, but with a price tag of €150 each, sadly my dream of wearing a different *sevillana* dress every day of my life was not about to be realised. There was room for only one in my life and as soon as I laid eyes on a luscious, sky-blue dress with big white spots, white-trimmed frills and cascading white lace, I knew we were meant to be.

A simple white *pico*, or small triangular shawl, crisp white shoes and white dangly earrings would have complimented the ensemble beautifully but were not in keeping with the custom of making *sevillana* outfits so lurid they could be seen from outer space. Instead, the shop assistant showed me how to amp up the luminosity by wrapping clashing shawls of garish orange, tomato-red or off-green around my shoulders. Bizarrely, they all worked but with the prices the store was charging for shawls, I could have flown return to China and bought some freshly made. In the end, I profusely thanked my new fairy godmother for her assistance and, with my stunning new purchase in hand, left to shop for accessories elsewhere.

The first item on the agenda? A fan.

The *abanico*, or small hand fan, has been a staple in Spanish culture for at least a couple of centuries when it progressed from being a status symbol into a nifty way to keep cool in the stifling summer months. Their most creative use, however, can be traced back to the Golden Age of Flamenco. Back in the late 19th century, single women weren't allowed to mingle with the opposite sex without a chaperone watching their every move (which, if you weren't a closet *lesbiana* must have put a bit of a dampener on things). To overcome such austerity, the *señoritas* of the time apparently developed a secret language using their fans that only they and their suitors could understand. (Their chaperones clearly weren't the brightest of people.)

Their covert signals were brilliant. Depending on which research you delve into, moving a fan slowly over your chest may have meant: '*I'm single and ready to mingle*,' which was not to be confused with fluttering a fan quickly and in short sweeps across your chest to signal: '*Bugger off, I'm taken*.' An open fan that touched your cheek (on your face) told someone you liked them, whilst resting a closed fan on your left cheek basically gave someone the green light to get jiggy with you.

A typical scenario could have unfolded (pun intended) as such: a girl walked into a dance with her fan in her left hand, hit the same hand with her fan, opened her fan over her chin, reopened and closed her fan then pointed it, before she opened her fan over her left ear, placed the fan over her mouth, slowly closed the fan, placed the closed fan near her heart, then fiddled with it (the fan, not her heart). What the bleep had she just said?! Simple: '*I want a boyfriend. I like you. I want to talk to you. Meet me over there but don't tell anyone. Kiss me. I promise to marry you. I love you. Now hurry up!*'

If the girl's Romeo remained clueless, or was merely short-sighted, she would have immediately undertaken the following actions: touched her nose with the fan, hit the fan on her dress, opened and closed the fan, hit the fan on her right hand, covered her face with the fan, twirled the fan in her right hand, then closed it behind her head – which would have basically let him have it, fan-style: *'Something stinks here. I'm jealous and upset. I don't like you. It's over between us! I love another. Forget me not.'*

Single ladies had no time to waste in those days.

At least I understood why I was never asked out after a performance of the one and only dance I knew how to perform with a fan – a sensual little number known as a *guajira*. With so many flirty fan signals embedded in the choreography, I'd given out way too many mixed signals.

In those early student years, getting my hands on a *pericón*, or large wooden-framed fan, in order to learn the *guajira* was almost as challenging as the dance itself. After weeks of searching, all I managed to rustle up was a heavy, red-and-green, dragon-embossed fan from Brisbane's Chinatown. As my fellow students coquettishly flicked open their elegantly dainty designs, I cumbersomely wrenched mine open to the sound of a thunderous fart noise. At least everyone knew when I was in time though.

Down another Sevillian side street, with my new blue-spotty dress in tow, I discovered a beautiful store devoted entirely to flamenco accessories. What were the odds?! Considering it was Andalucía, probably very high. Amongst vividly coloured hair combs and Jennifer Lopez-style hoop earrings so big they could carry my shopping home, I almost forgot why I was there. Finally, in my best Spanish, I asked the shop assistant if she would select three wooden fabric fans from the display cabinet for me in gentle *azul*, sunny *amarillo* and dazzlingly bright *blanco*.

'*¿Quieres una bolsa?*' the shop assistant asked as I fished my wallet out of my front pocket.

'Huh?' I raised my eyebrows.

'*¿Quieres una bolsa?*' she repeated.

'Um. *¿Qué?*'

'*¿¿QUIERES UNA BOLSA?!*'

I don't think the shop assistant realised continually repeating a phrase that had been so woefully misunderstood the first time around would lead to any further enlightenment.

'*Lo siento, no entiendo.*' I pulled the ignorance card.

The now surly shop assistant glared at me and blurted out in angry staccatoed English, 'DO. JU. WANT. A. BAG?!'

The chances of me ever misunderstanding that phrase again are *cero*.

16

IMPROVISACIÓN IMPULSIVA
The Spice of Spontaneity

It all happened so fast. Just as I was beginning to harmonise with the quirky cadences of Seville, it was almost time to leave. The following afternoon I would be heading south to Jerez de la Frontera to attend their annual flamenco festival and spend an entire week bathing in the heavenly aura of a certain Ángel. That left just a few hours to be *una local* and wander the Sevillian streets, salivating over decadent costume designs whilst I fended off pickpockets. It was also my last opportunity to avail myself of the free toilets at McDonald's and El Corte Inglés, and the very final time I would be shouted at by tourist boats along the River Guadalquivir. I just wasn't ready to leave.

I attended all three dance classes, determined to soak up every last drop of inspired sweat. It had taken only two weeks of intensive dance lessons and private rehearsals – give or take several lessons and rehearsals – to have finally felt flamenco fit and ready for Ángel.

'*Quiero una foto, por favor?*' I asked Isabel after our last lesson together.

'*Sí, sí.*' Isabel happily posed with me. I would have loved to have captured her looks of benevolent bewilderment as well, but somehow knew she wouldn't be the only teacher ever to dish them out to me.

With no chance of seeing the great Paco de Lucía in concert (who was alive and well but touring elsewhere at the time), I turned my attention to another gifted local guitarist. For days, I'd been seeing posters advertising his upcoming show, which just so happened to coincide with my last night in Seville. The only way to purchase tickets was in person at the theatre's box office but every time I moseyed on over, it was closed. On my fourth attempt, it was miraculously open but I was informed by the box office staff that tickets would not go on sale until the day of the performance. Finally, that day had arrived.

After Isabel's lesson, I raced into town and purchased a single ticket for the show. Having already exceeded my budget for the day, I then bought a lime-green shawl that clashed wildly with my blue-and-white *sevillana* dress, before hot-footing it back to the hotel to soak my feet and doll myself up for the evening.

At long last I finally found where all the cute boys hung out: the theatre! In the foyer before the show were throngs of brooding, budding guitarists and flirty, male *aficionados*. With the ratio of gorgeous guys to girls being 20:1, I was glad I'd at least combed my hair for the occasion. Somehow, the aforementioned hotties managed to score better tickets than me as I ended up in the nosebleed section of the upper balcony – where leg room and oxygen were an afterthought. But once the incomparable and kindly looking guitarist took to the stage, it didn't matter where anyone was for the sold-out performance, just so long as you were there.

¡What a show! ¡What a guitarist! The level of playing was not only flawless but enchanting, complimented beautifully by the insanely talented musicians in his band. Together, the hotties and I were taken on a magical journey of *música*, zest and joy. It was so thoroughly mesmerising, I was caught completely unawares when a tall, lean, middle-aged dancer in an audaciously simple dress and green suede shoes took to the stage. When she threw herself into a ferocious, confronting display of raw *emoción* from the throbbing depths of her aching spirit, I was plunged deep into culture shock and sat with my mouth agape as the dancer performed wild, writhing turns and frenzied footwork with unapologetic in-your-face intensity.

For the next piece, the *bailaora* appeared in a fluffy, white terry towelling-inspired *bata de cola* lined with blue ribbons, under which she wore bright purple shoes. It was an ingenious way to soak up sweat. Understandably, not only could the ardently appreciative audience not get enough of her, but neither could the guitarist who watched her every move with unabashed delight. It was only *afterwards* that I found out that they were, in fact, married. *Claro.*

After the concert, Sebastian invited me to meet up with him and a posse of his friends at a nearby bar. Sebastian hadn't been to the performance – I assumed because it cost money – but a number of his mates had and were raving about it. Unfortunately, my voracious appetite took precedence over my shy reluctance to engage with strangers and, as everyone compared notes from the show, I occupied myself trying to identify the ingredients in a weird fishy excuse for a *tapas* dish.

Mateo, the hip-thrusting, Italian busker from Betanzo's class then joined in the fray, alongside two young barely European women and their dog – whom I was tempted to give the rest of my supper to (the dog, not the women). I bravely tried striking up a conversation with one of the English-speaking girls to find out if she was into flamenco, but all I received in return was admonishment for not speaking Spanish.

'It iz ze only way you will learn! You have to zpeak only in Zpanish. No English, Zpanish! All ze time!' Miss Spanish Inquisition spat at me in between puffs on a joint. Had I not spent forever working around the clock to pay for the trip of a lifetime, I might have had time to increase my vocabulary from more than 20 words but since I was only in the country for a month, half of which had already transpired, she could get the @#$% over herself. I was not going to spend my last night in Seville in *indignación*, being reprimanded by some irate pothead who probably also berated her dog for not barking with rolled 'r's.

'I'm outta here, Seb!' I shouted across the bar and stormed back towards Triana.

It was just after midnight. As I passed through the outskirts of town, a busking slide guitarist paused to enjoy a cigarette. Across the road, things were altogether a different matter, however. Thirty men with white towels wrapped around their heads were crouched motionless under a barren festival float. Were they a terry towelling tribute band rehearsing for Carnaval? Bemused, I stood and waited for them to lift the float above their heads but, alas, all 30 men stayed crouched under the float, stationary and silent, as if trying to hide in plain sight. Perhaps it was a good thing I was leaving Seville after all.

17

MARCANDO
On the Move

Out of everything in Seville, I was going to miss Manuel the most. I'd never encountered such unwavering passion on a daily basis before. To offer my final respects – and so as not to get singled out – I poured every last surge of energy into conquering both choreographies, and even managed to ace a tricky *escobilla* section with a completely numb toe. Throughout both classes Manuel beamed proudly at my progress, which sent my confidence into the stratosphere.

When the final lesson was over, I hurled my camera at Sebastian and myself at Manuel and requested in broken Spanish if I could get a photo.

'*Por supuesto.*' Manuel smiled. I hoped my eyes conveyed my heartfelt appreciation of being able to learn from him for the fortnight, because my language certainly didn't.

There was no time to plunge any unresponsive extremities into an ice bath back at the hotel. Sebastian was already waiting in the lobby by the time my backpack and I made it downstairs and together, we walked towards the central train station where we were to meet up with two of our dearest friends before we all travelled to Jerez. As there was a fair bit of ground to cover between Triana and the station, Sebastian kindly offered to carry my backpack. I had the straps undone before he'd even finished asking. Someone else's pants could fall down for a change.

'Aren't we going straight to Santa Justa?' I asked when Sebastian took a detour off the main drag.

'We will once we pick up Abigail.'

'Oh, I didn't realise she was joining us.'

Maybe it was a French thing but by the time we trekked over to her apartment, Abigail had stockpiled about 200 suitcases on the footpath outside – which meant walking to the train station on foot was no longer *viable*. While Sebastian looked around for a taxi, Abigail informed me she was putting on a big flamenco show in her hometown. She had so much flamenco knick-knackery, one suitcase alone held over 100 synthetic roses. It sounded like quite the spectacle, akin to four people crammed into a Spanish cab gasping for air as they balanced hundreds of French suitcases on their laps.

When we finally arrived at Santa Justa station, Sebastian tumbled out of the taxi and started wrestling with the luggage, which prompted Abigail to ask me in hushed tones if I would split the cab fare with her since our mutual friend was unemployed. Technically so was I, I wanted to protest. The last of my work contracts had been done and dusted well before I left Australia and if we hadn't had to fork out for a freaking cab to ferry all of her @#$% luggage around, we would've just walked to the train station. Begrudgingly, I handed over half the fare.

'Staaaaace!!!!!' Evie hurled herself at me from across the train platform; her tousled, scarlet hair flying defiantly behind her. 'How the fark are ya, mate?!' she shrieked as her slender frame enveloped me in a fierce hug.

Before I could answer with any kind of eloquence, I was bowled over by the lanky Madelyn. 'So good to see you, Stace!!' she exclaimed; her rich, expressive blue eyes dancing merrily from beneath her sleek, stylish black bob. Both girls looked like they'd stepped straight from the pages of a fashion magazine, rather than their respective international flights. 'I'm so happy to see you guys!' I gushed and held on tightly to them both.

'Hey, save some for me.' A voice chuckled from behind.

'Seb!!!!!!' the girls cried out, instantly enfolding him into their embrace.

'We're so happy to be here! It's been a farking adventure getting to this point, let me tell you.' Evie's green eyes twinkled mischievously. 'But if we don't get a wriggle on, we might miss the farking train!'

She had a point.

By the time we boarded the carriage, all of the seats had been taken, so we copied every other flamenco student en route to Jerez and slumped down on the floor, squashed together like *sardinas*. Sebastian thought it would be hilarious if we took photos of ourselves with scarves wrapped around our heads pretending to be *gitanos*. He became slightly annoyed when he saw we'd been smiling in all of the shots. 'You're supposed to be poor, sad *gitanas*!' he exclaimed indignantly. With my good friends in tow, an upcoming workshop with Ángel and a two-week flamenco festival to look forward to, it was *imposible* to be morose.

Once we arrived in Jerez, technically we could have walked from the train station to the accommodation my friends and I had booked near the centre of town, but it wouldn't have been fair to ask Sebastian to carry all of our luggage there. Wisely, he hailed us a cab instead.

As the taxi turned into Calle Cartuja, all eyes were immediately drawn to a very striking centerpiece in the middle of a roundabout: a headless, armless statue of a man with rippling pectorals and an enviable six pack doing his best impersonation of a gnarled oak tree. At 13 metres high, he was pretty hard to miss.

I'd assumed the headless hottie was a tribute to Ángel and was somewhat surprised to hear the sculpture was actually a mythological Minotaur. As the fable went, the muscly monolith was dismembered in a fight in a maze on the island of Crete, towards which he still leaned. Mister Minotaur may have valiantly tried to escape a labyrinth, but he wasn't able to outrun footy fever. Not long after our visit, the statue was outfitted in giant, blue-and-white sporting apparel courtesy of the local Xerez Deportivo soccer club – and wouldn't you know it? For the first time in 62 years, the team won its division.

'This is it, guys! Our new home!' I enthused as we pulled up outside the apartment complex Evie, Madelyn and I would be sharing for the following two weeks. As we walked through the main gate, our landlords – a middle-aged couple and their cute, friendly dog – welcomed us like long-lost friends. Sebastian bade us farewell and continued on in the taxi to his uncle's place, where I assumed his uncle had his wallet ready.

With its proximity to the festival, and its not too obscenely overpriced tariffs, our new lodgings could not have been more ideal: three self-contained, ground-floor apartments that converged into a cosy, central courtyard above which the owners lived. Had there been a pool in the vicinity, we would have sworn it was Melrose Place.

The moment I stepped into my combined lounge/kitchen/dining room, I was welcomed with a big cheery basket of dried, dead wheat. Whether I was expected to mill my own flour and open a makeshift bakery whilst I was in town was not immediately apparent but, on closer inspection, the dastardly harvest turned out to be lavender.

Tucked behind the kitchenette was a compact little bathroom without a bathtub – which meant no more handwashing. *¡Olé!* (I gave the landlords' washing machine a workout instead.) Throwing my backpack into the huge, colourful bedroom at the end of the hallway, I began to search, in vain, for the free welcome bottle of sherry the website I booked through had promised. After 10 minutes of fruitless rummaging, I conceded that either a) the website had lied or, b) Evie had found the sherry first. At least if I was ever bored stiff with sobriety, there were a few more television channels on offer.

'*Burrrrrp!*' Evie poked her flaming red hair through the front door of my apartment. 'You almost ready, mate? Wow, nice digs!' she declared, stepping inside. 'This is much bigger than ours!'

Madelyn appeared next. 'Whoa, this is huge, Stace! You scored big time!'

With Evie staying only the first week of the festival, she and Madelyn were bunking down in the central unit together, leaving me to lounge in unabashed luxury in my own little slice of paradise. A Swedish flamenco student by the name of Markus had rented out the remaining apartment beside us, but the girls and I would have to wait until he arrived the following day to ascertain whether he was straight – and single.

'Do you reckon we'll need jackets?' I asked Evie as we headed out to celebrate the opening night of the festival.

'Who the fark knows, mate?' She shrugged.

On our way to meet Simone, our much-loved, statuesque, Julia Roberts-looking flamenco teacher from Brisbane, Madelyn, Evie and I accidentally bumped into her as she was staying only a few streets away. As we all strolled towards the centre of town, Simone joked about how every time she walked through her communal courtyard, her overly zealous landlord would instantly appear and want to spend the next day and a half conversing with her. Simone was fluent in Spanish so language was no barrier but neither, according to her landlord, was time.

We were in great hands with Simone. She'd been frequenting the festival for so many years, she knew all of the best places to visit – one of which was a convivial local watering hole close to all the action. We were just tucking into some ruby red *vinos* at the bar when Sebastian appeared and enthusiastically reunited with his former teacher.

Any way you looked at it, the Festival de Jerez was a pretty sweet deal. Every February, anyone who was anybody in the professional flamenco world ascended to the voluptuous town of Jerez to run weeklong workshops by day and debut their latest productions by night. International dance, guitar and singing students of every calibre could attend and, the best part was, once you'd paid for a workshop, you automatically received a free ticket to the big-name flamenco shows held in the Teatro Villamarta every night.

By the time we arrived at the majestic Teatro, flocks of flamenco dancers (please don't ever refer to them as flamingo dancers unless you want to sustain long-term injuries) were already congregating outside. It quickly became apparent that there was no point ever arriving any earlier at the theatre to grab a drink or find your seat, because you would never be let in. Only when there was five minutes left until show time, theatre staff would fling open the main doors, through which only a handful of ushers checked the tickets of 1,226 patrons, who were then left entirely to their own devices to find their seats. It was daringly brave and yet, somehow, it always seemed to work.

Once inside the two-tiered theatre, the girls and I split up to find our allocated seats for the week. I was overjoyed when I found mine in plum position in the stalls (nothing to do with having booked Ángel's workshop the second online tickets went on sale the previous year, I was sure). Much to my delight, and hopefully hers, Simone was seated behind me.

Opening the festival was world-famous flamenco export Eva Yerbabuena, winner of just about every Spanish dance award in existence. She was also the first flamenco performer ever nominated in the National UK Dance Awards. In her homeland, however, she wasn't known as Eva but was reverently referred to as the "Queen of the Soleá" – the *soleá* being a dark, sombre flamenco *palo* that was as agonising as it was intense. (On a lighter note, her stage surname meant peppermint, which certainly refreshed proceedings somewhat.)

Eva was premiering her brand new production *Lluvia*, or "Rain" and described the performance as her most personal yet, in which she would be reflecting her true essence under a cloak of *melancolía*. The first half was certainly that with weighty song choices and grey, solemn lighting – all of which evoked an ethereal sense of isolation and despair that provided a stunning contrast for when the clouds began to part.

To show off her comical side, in the second act Eva dressed up as if she was going to Carnaval and exaggeratedly shook her hips to an amusing *tanguillo de Cádiz*, followed by a quick costume change for a jovial *alegría*. For the finale, however, Eva had saved the best for last. In a jet-black *bata de cola* she performed a regally impressive *soleá*. Her stage presence was so commanding that watching her felt like being caught in the eye of a fierce storm. To end the show, Queen Eva flung off her shoes and walked through the adoring crowd.

Had I been in closer proximity, I would have offered her a mint.

18

DUENDE
The Flamenco X Factor

One could just imagine how light and breezy Jerez apartments were in summer with their cool, white floor tiles and open-aired ambiance. Residing in them in winter, however, was akin to living in a flimsy tent deep in the Antarctic whilst wearing nothing but a silk nightie – an interesting notion in theory but a hypothermic, nipple-freezing practice in reality. You knew it was cold when your breath turned to vapour before you even got out of bed.

'Stace! How'd ya sleep, mate?' Evie asked as I stumbled out into the sun-dappled courtyard where the girls were warming their hands on piping hot cups of coffee.

'Not too well, Evie, but I'll get there.'

'Just drink more sherry, mate. Warm yourself up then knock yourself out.'

'Or get sloshed on some of that *sangría* you bought,' Madelyn suggested. After the Teatro show, the girls and I had stopped by the local supermarket. Not only was the store about five times the size of my former little corner store in Triana, it was way more expensive and stocked completely different brands, which instantly made me homesick for Seville. (Once I discovered its liquor department sold casks of *sangría* at €2 a pop, however, I began to warm to the place.)

Ratatata tat.

I bounded over to see who was knocking on the front gate and found myself face-to-face with a tall, blonde drink of Swedish water.

'*Hola*. I'm Markus.' The booming, broad-shouldered man introduced himself.

'Markus! Oh hi, I'm Stacey!' I shook his hand as he entered the courtyard. 'This is Madelyn.'

'And I'm Evie!' Evie jumped up and greeted him with a hug. 'Markus, hey?' She looked him up and down approvingly. 'How the fark are ya?'

Markus laughed, revealing a Tim Curry-esque smile. 'Nice to meet you all. Where are you ladies from? Australia?' he asked as he took a seat.

'Got it in one, mate,' Evie declared proudly, before demonstrating how loudly she could burp.

Markus looked a little taken aback. 'You don't happen to know Sebastian, do you?'

'Seb?! Yeah! He's our good mate! We hung out with him last night and we all used to do flamenco together!' we responded.

'I met him at last year's festival. Such great company! So which workshops are you doing this week?'

'Evie and I are learning from Ángel,' I volunteered.

'Me too!' Markus nodded, his blue eyes dancing in the light.

'Now I wish I was.' Madelyn sighed. 'I'm doing *bata de cola* with Ángeles someone or other.'

'At least we're all going to be learning from angels,' I offered.

'Do you know how to get to these workshops?' Evie asked.

'Yes actually, Ángel's teaching in the same studio as last year.'

'You mean you've learnt from him before?' My eyes widened exponentially.

'I have and he was that good, I'm back for more.' Markus laughed as Madelyn handed him a copy of the class timetable. 'Okay, let's see here. Right, the studio you'll be going to is on the way to Ángel's,' Markus explained to Madelyn. 'I'll walk you there on the way to our workshop this afternoon. Let me get settled in now but *hasta luego*, ladies. I'll see you after lunch.' Markus smiled and disappeared into his apartment.

Whenever I lost my bearings in Seville, a network of cobblestoned alleyways, pigeons and limbless beggars would inevitably steer me back towards the major arterials. From there, all I had to do was follow the trail of ringing church bells, bustling *tapas* bars and pushy tourist boats to find my way back to Triana. But in the enigmatic elevations of Jerez, roads not only wound around but up and down; some of which led me further astray, others which took me to places where I felt like *I* was the tourist attraction.

Thank goodness for Markus, our trusty knight in shining flamenco boots who, as promised, masterfully steered the girls and me through the slippery, rain-soaked streets of Jerez to deliver us to our respective dance studios. As I tentatively climbed the stairs of the Gimnasio Mantara, it finally hit me. The dream of spending an entire week feasting my eyes and ears upon Ángel was about to become a reality. So what did I do? I freaked out and fled to the bathroom.

I'd had six months to prepare for that moment, but clearly hadn't factored in how long it would take my shaking hands to shed all of my bulky, wintery layers and slip into my hot, new red-and-black dance ensemble – before I visited the loo several times, of course. By the time I walked into the studio, the warm-ups had begun. *¡¡#@$%!!* Not only had I missed Ángel's all-important introduction and created my own tardy version, but the notorious problem with workshops was students were creatures of habit. Whichever position they found themselves in on the first day would be where they would steadfastly remain for the rest of the week.

Not wanting to draw any further attention to myself, I scuttled to the other side of the studio, offered a sheepish hi to Sharon (the last of my friends from Brisbane) and took a spot in the second back row in front of Evie, who seemed determined not to draw any attention to herself for the *entire* workshop.

Sebastian had an ongoing theory about the type of students Ángel's workshops attracted and predicted we would be surrounded by mostly females of the predominantly older – and predominantly German – persuasion. Sure enough, as soon as the first '*Schnell*' echoed around the room, I looked around to discover the class was filled to the brim with *Hausfrauen*; the majority of whom appeared never to have worn a high heel in their life, let alone danced in one.

There were so many of them, they blocked the view of Ángel and, for most of the warm-ups, Evie, Sharon and I were forced to mimic the students directly in front of us. (Markus had the foresight to secure a spot in the front row.) In utter frustration, I began pounding my feet harder and harder into the impervious floor when, all of a sudden, the sea of inept students parted and I caught my first Spanish glimpse of Ángel; mid-thigh lunge, his tree trunk-size quadriceps rippling through his trousers, whilst a mop of dark, curly hair fell in sexy ringlets around his face. The workshop paid for itself then and there.

When Ángel demonstrated the opening steps of the dance we were to learn, he kept winking at a particular student in the front row. Did he know her? Had she won a competition to receive extra privileges or something? Then, just as soon as he'd made her feel like she was the only woman in the world, Ángel turned his ocular attentions to someone else. It almost became a dance in itself: teach a step, wink at some lucky student, teach another step, wink at another grateful recipient.

Mental Note #1: Ángel is an outrageous flirt.

It didn't take long to notice that the students who received the most attention were the bungling old *Damen* in distress.

They might not have known the difference between their *plantas* (balls of the foot) and their *tacones* (heels), but they sure were proficient at amassing every single one of Ángel's eye flutters. They deserved some credit though. Enrolling in an expensive flamenco course in another country, for which they'd dusted off a pair of moth-bitten dance shoes they'd once bought at a second-hand store, then acting helplessly smug whilst a hot Spanish Adonis doted on their every move was rather cunning.

It was game on, biddies.

When the students were all warmed up – both from the exercise and internal hot flushes – Ángel explained in very broken English that the *palo* he would be teaching us for the week was a *martinete*: the very first dance I had seen him perform with Paco Peña back in Brisbane. We definitely had our work cut out for us. *Martinetes* were from the *cante jondo* family of flamenco: intensely sad songs believed to have originated with the blacksmiths, borne out of the intense persecution and hardship they suffered. Although *martinetes* were traditionally sung to the sound of a hammer striking an anvil, they had since evolved into a popular style of dance. A *cantaor* (singer) and *palmero* (clapper) would be joining us towards the end of the week but, until then, it was just Ángel and 30 of his most devoted, and mostly female, students. I hoped he had security.

For a very powerful and intoxicating dancer, Ángel was also a complete clown. To begin with, Ángel had us practise the *martinete* rhythm by clapping out the accented 12-beat *compás*. Once we settled into a groove, he rewarded us by dancing a comical little jig. On another occasion, whilst he repeatedly demonstrated a new step to one of the clueless old maids, Ángel over-exaggerated by flapping his arms about, wiggling his hips and knocking his knees together like an absolute goofball. It was beyond endearing.

Towards the end of the lesson, I must have subconsciously hammed it up. That, or my arms had genuinely taken on a life of their own but, within seconds of spotting my sincere struggles, Ángel was by my side and ready to assist. Once he confirmed which language I spoke (the language of love was sadly not an option), his arms were around mine fashioning them into graceful, grateful wings as a crimson flush flitted across my face.

Mental Note #2: Wear a lower cut top to the second class.

It was *Día de Andalucía*: a public holiday that commemorated the right of the southern Andalucían province to run as an autonomous, self-governing region. To celebrate, every licensed premise in Jerez was well and truly open for business. Downing a sherry, or 10, with Sharon, Evie and Markus at a nearby café after class provided a welcome respite from watching television with my feet soaked in a bucket of icy water whilst I munched my way through a bag of *patatas fritas*. Being the luminescent lightweight that I was, however, I was forced to line my stomach first and kicked off proceedings with my first ever authentic plate of *patatas*

alioli. In Spanish-themed restaurants throughout Australia, this classic dish is served as a hot, creamy, garlicky potato casserole but in Jerez, or at least in that particular bar, it was more like a potato salad – cold and chunky; some would say a little like me during winter.

The excitement of reuniting with friends, my new surroundings, the first class with Ángel and the free-flowing liquor soon caught up with me and, before I knew it, I was back at the apartment, snuggled into bed for an afternoon *siesta*. I was just nodding off when Markus began hammering out footwork on the tiled floor of his lounge room, conveniently located a metre away from my head. It turned out to be a very efficient way to practise the *martinete* rhythms without having to get out of bed.

Ángel not only heroically spent the first day of the workshop winking at incompetent *sauerkrauts*, but he was also starring in a major production at the Teatro that evening alongside dancer Adela Campallo (Rafa's sister), whose skirt-shredding class Sebastian and I observed back in Seville.

'What the freak?!'

Madelyn, Evie, Markus and I were on our way to the pre-show bar when we unwittingly found ourselves caught up in the midst of a lively street parade. Hundreds of spectators were crowded onto footpaths as a string of motorised floats swept by. Admiration soon turned into astonishment when we noticed that every float contained only young children enthusiastically prancing about and dancing to live renditions of "I Will Survive". It was like an inappropriate Carnaval for Kids. We lasted only a couple of minutes.

After a few too many sherries, the gang and I poured ourselves into the Teatro ready to be inspired by *Inspiración*: a showcase for local guitarist Juan Diego's upcoming album, to which Ángel and Adela had choreographed dances to match. Usually in flamenco, it was the other way around – a guitarist followed the singer or dancer's lead but *tradición* was about to be well and truly thrown out of the Teatro's wine bottle-shaped windows.

Props to Juan – he had managed to assemble the largest flamenco band in existence. Aside from himself, there were two singers, an electric guitarist, a percussionist, two *palmeros* and a trumpet player who also dabbled in flugelhorn. It was a bold, brassy move but in Spain, the process of modernising and fusing flamenco with unique instrumentation had been occurring for decades. In contrast in Australia, women performing in trousers was about as controversial as it got.

When the show commenced, a rogue student snuck into the empty seat on the other side of me. Whether she was profoundly deaf or extravagantly passionate, I could not immediately discern but the second she slapped her hands together to show her appreciation, she was instantly in the running to be crowned "The Loudest Palmera of Europe". Her claps were so ear-piercing, they put an air rifle to shame.

Just as I was considering ducking to the bar to stick some serviettes in my ear, Ángel burst onstage in a shimmering burgundy long-sleeved shirt (with trousers, sadly). Not to be outdone, his dance partner wore a lovely matching burgundy long-sleeved dress with diagonal ruffles and layers of white lace. It would be the first of Adela's six costume changes for the evening and *por qué no*? Even though she was an incredible dancer in her own right, she had to do something to take the focus off Ángel every now and then. Together, the duo launched into a jaunty *bulería*, followed by a sombre *seguiriya*, after which time Adela really showed what she was made of with a dramatic *soleá por bulería*.

In a black-collared shirt and black velvet jacket (sadly, with pants again), Ángel then lightened proceedings with a lively *rumba* and *alegría*; the perfect sunny vehicles to show off his cheeky chops. Then, so as not to lull the audience into a false sense of security that that was as good as flamenco could ever get, Spain abruptly unleashed its secret weapon: Tomasito.

A tall, lanky man reminiscent of Klinger from *Mash* – but without women's clothing – swaggered onto the stage and began speaking to the audience. He then had a bit of a boogie, followed by another chat and then wriggled around some more. During another one of his numbers, Tomasito held up a sign that read '*Fino*', meaning fine. Was he judging his own performance or Ángel's behind? Regardless, his lyrics had the crowd in hysterics and me in complete bewilderment as he sang, rhymed and wiggled his way around with pure, unadulterated aplomb.

Forget trying to categorise the man, Tomasito gave new meaning to the word *original*. He was neither a traditional singer, dancer nor professional clown, but fell somewhere in the category of a comic-dancing beat poet with razor-sharp timing and charisma that would put even George Clooney to shame. As a youngster, Tomasito was equally inspired by flamenco as he was by jazz, rock, hip-hop, Led Zeppelin and Michael Jackson. With such a wide range of influences, Tomasito vowed never to be confined and successfully blazed his own unique career path, ignoring the naysayers in favour of just doing what he and his body felt like doing.

Bless his funky socks. In the early 2000s, Tomasito put his money where his mouth was and released a flamenco rap album; the cover of which was a photo of him in his underwear.

Respeto.

19

CASTAÑUELAS
Ow My Freaking Ears

Ángel was in top form during the second lesson with his *personalidad carismática* in full flight. Soon after the workshop started, he became so frustratingly bemused when he forgot how a particular step went, he staged a mock dramatic nervous breakdown and collapsed, pretending to cry on one of the German biddies who wasted no time in offering him her heaving, Helga-esque bosom for support. In another section of choreography, Ángel exaggerated one of the steps so much that it morphed into "The Chicken Dance". *Touché* was all I could say, given the class demographics.

Later, as we practised new footwork, Ángel made a beeline straight for me. Just the thought of him even glancing in my direction usually made me lose my *concentración*, but I was so determined to demonstrate that at least one of his students could actually dance (apart from Markus and my friends, that was), I stared straight ahead and forced myself to maintain focus.

'*Eso es.*' He complimented me before moving on. It was the same phrase Manuel had directed my way. What's more, I even caught a wink from Ángel later on – once I discovered the secret to catching one was to shove all the other students aside and stare unblinkingly at him whenever he swept his gaze across the room.

My happy disposition was short-lived, however, as many of the attendees were still struggling with the simplest of steps; bumping and ricocheting off each other like mindless buffoons. Although the workshop level was *básico*, or beginners, it should have still demanded students had *some* flamenco dance experience. The festival did offer *iniciación* for complete novices, but I assumed hot, winking Spanish men weren't running those workshops.

After class, spurred on by the official "flamenco trail" touted in the festival programme, Madelyn and I wandered off in search of flamenco apparel. Although we didn't manage to find a single ruffle, what we accidentally discovered was much more enticing. Tucked in the hills behind the centre of town was an otherworldly *tetería*, or Moorish tea house, that served up heady Arabic coffee and exotic herbal teas in its warm, cavernous interior.

'This is the life, Mads,' I mused as I sipped on a piquant cup of rooibos tea.

'I know where I'm having breakfast from now on,' Madelyn concurred as she tucked into a delectable serving of chocolate-flavoured crepes.

A long, hot shower would have rounded off the afternoon delightfully, were it not for the fact that the shower cubicle in my apartment also doubled as a Houdini contraption. In Jerez, water drainage was on Spain time and never in any hurry to disappear down the plughole. Showering became a race against time to get adequately cleaned before water filled the shallow recess and threatened to flood the bathroom floor. It was a pretty crafty way of enforcing two-minute showers.

Having never experienced *escuela bolera* prior to arriving in Jerez, I hadn't known how lucky I'd been. Once I'd witnessed it live at the festival, however, I was happy if I never experienced it again.

Escuela bolera is a combination of classical ballet and flamenco – flamenco ballet, if you will – a theatrical style of performance where dancers dress in traditional costumes and perform to pre-recorded orchestral music (which doesn't sound too bad). Although flamenco shoes don't get a look in (women wear slippers and men wear mute boots), with all the incredible leaps, bounds and spins the dancers perform that's probably a good thing. Visually, there is no doubt that it's spectacular and full of incredible artistry. There is just one little infuriating component from which there is no audible escape – and that is the castanet.

Surprisingly, castanets never originated in Spain but, just like the percussive *cajón*, have become inextricably fused with flamenco as the art form has evolved. There's no one singular culture to blame for their introduction either. Castanets have been linked to the Phoenicians, Greeks, Romans, Moors and Chinese, but what has made them such a staple instrument in Spain is the country's refusal to stop playing them. Now, I'm all for the occasional little flutter but nonstop clackers drive me crackers.

It has been said that if you practise castanets every day of your life, not only will you become profoundly deaf but it will take you that long just to master a roll. Whether you call them *castañuelas*, *pulgaretes* or *palillos*, the truth is they are bloody hard to master and require both hands to be completely independent of the other due to each castanet having a different tone. The left castanet, known as the male, or *macho*, is lower in pitch than its partner and usually in charge of keeping the beat. The right hand holds the female, or *hembra*: a higher-pitched castanet used for tapping out intricate rhythms and rolls.

Forget those cheat versions of castanets on sticks, or the dodgy little blue-and-red ones from primary school days, authentic clackers involve looping a thick thread of rope around each thumb and hitting the outer edge of the wooden or fibreglass castanet with a single finger, allowing the two halves to slap together and bounce open before the next finger has a go. Once you master the basics, you have to learn to play the suckers at the speed of light in order to produce any kind of consistent clickety-clackety sound. You can then mix it up a little by smacking each castanet together to produce a satisfying loud 'THWACK' noise or, my personal favourite, repeatedly hitting yourself in the upper arm with a castanet from the opposite hand; a trick you can continue up and down your arm for hours to great acclaim, and impressive bruising.

But be warned. Every one of those skills becomes obsolete once you lift your arms and try to dance with the darned things. Any slight deviation from your castanet facing downwards and it will close up like a clam, refusing to make another clickety or a clack. Adding counter-rhythm footwork, spins and circling arms will really test your sanity, as will trying to play them in perfect unison with a dance partner during a *sevillana* (especially if you're both dancing a different numbered version).

Really, was it any wonder the Catholic Church temporarily banned the playing of castanets in the early 1700s because they insinuated mayhem and rebellion? Priests wouldn't have been able to hear anyone's confessions over the racket.

Somehow, despite all of the above, my ears and I made it to the end of my first and last ever *escuela bolera* show. During the final bows, Loud Clapping Lady leant over and said that hearing all the castanets had made her want to learn them. I nodded vigorously, assuming she had said *burn* them.

20

JUERGA
¡Party Time!

Right on cue, the 8 a.m. wakeup call I had not requested – in the form of jackhammering and metal grinding from the construction site next door – roused me from the deepest of slumbers. Although rain had been forecast for the week, there would be no reprieve from the noise as the entire worksite was conveniently located undercover. So much for booking the apartment under the pretense that it was located in a quiet part of Jerez. Just like the free bottle of sherry that had been promised on arrival, I was beginning to realise there was no such thing.

'Ready to go, Stace?' Madelyn was at my front door.

'On my way, Mads!' I hollered out from the bedroom as I zipped up the last of my wintery layers.

'Hopefully we'll find some flamenco shops this time around,' Madelyn suggested as we exited the courtyard.

'If not, we could always stock up on more of that cask *sangría*.'

For the second week of the festival, Madelyn and I had enrolled in a *mantón* dance workshop and, with the long-limbed Madelyn already the proud owner of a substantial shawl of her own, I was fast running out of time to get my mittens on a suitably shimmering creation. There had been plenty on offer in Seville, I just hadn't been emotionally ready to part with €98 at the time.

Mantones were yet another modern addition to flamenco repertoire. When the first silk shawl was brought ashore by ship merchants in the 16th century, the women of Spain knew they'd happened upon a good thing when they saw them (the shawls, not the merchants – although I'm sure they were just as attractive in their own way). Ironically, even though the shawls known as *mantones de Manila* had been shipped from Manila, they'd been made in China. Once they'd arrived in Spain, however, it didn't take long for the shawls' traditionally embroidered Chinese dragons and pagoda designs to be replaced with more local floral embellishments and, brilliantly, it was the Sevillians who apparently came up with the idea of attaching fringing to the hems.

Defying common sense by looking for a *mantón* in a flamenco store, Madelyn and I wandered into a material shop, having been seduced by the plethora of spots in its window display. It wasn't the first time I'd been lured into such textile temptation. After my Emilio Estévez-inspired travels throughout North America, I'd made my way down to the south of Mexico (after missing my initial flight) to visit a dear friend. In the back streets of Tuxtla, we found a fabric warehouse packed to the rafters with hundreds of rolls of polka-dotted fabrics. Before anyone could sing "Chica Materialista", I'd snapped up metres of every white-, red- and black-spotted configuration on offer, with visions of turning them all into a dreamy, multi-layered flamenco dress. Almost a decade later, the material was still gathering dust under my bed because, quite frankly, I grew tired of that colour combination and didn't have the heart to be rejected by yet another dressmaker.

Back in Jerez, there may not have been any *mantones* in the fabric store, but there was a gorgeous selection of ready-made *boleros*, *sevillana* dresses and skirts. Since I'd succumbed to the slimming enfolds of my slinky new blue-and-white dress, I'd wanted more and instantly became infatuated with a luscious, black-and-white-spotted *sevillana* skirt priced at €80. Daring to be different, Madelyn became besotted with a garish, fluorescent-green outfit that wouldn't have been out of place in a Picasso museum. On my way to the checkout, I spied some sheer, silky, white-and-green fabric that would make a charming ruffled feature on a dress and jacket ensemble I wanted made. It wasn't long before that silky Spanish fabric ended up keeping the spotty Mexican material company under my bed.

It hadn't taken me long to commit flamenco sin in class. During the warm-ups, I spied a plum vacancy for *una estudiante* in the front row; a spot usually occupied by Mrs

Clogs – an old Dutch biddy who took her sweet time getting ready each day (well, longer than me). Without hesitation, I seized upon the piece of prime real estate before any other *oportunista* could.

Ángel was on everyone's case in class, making us practise the strenuous warm-ups over and over. You wouldn't stop in the middle of a performance, he explained, just because you were knackered. Neither should you stop when you were limbering up. The only way to get strong and stay strong, Ángel asserted, was to continually push yourself.

As most of the students would have done anything to gain his approval, we grinned and bore the fatigue, with our aching arms and shaking legs testimony to our collective persistence. Since I was in the front row, interactions with Ángel had exponentially increased and I watched with amusing *admiración* as he seamlessly switched from clowning around to commanding instant respect. During one exercise, he even sidled up and observed me hold a pose, before he comically mimed what it would look like if I stopped dancing mid-step, caught my breath and wiped my brow.

Unfortunately, he wasn't the only one watching me. As the lesson progressed, Mrs Clogs, who had positioned herself right behind me, began inching closer and closer until she was literally breathing down my neck. Her brilliant ploy backfired, however, as it only encouraged me to step further into Ángel's line of sight. Choreography came thick and fast during the lesson and, had I been ready to add any arms to the footwork, Mrs Clogs might have received a bit of a backhander.

The freezing, wet tiles of the apartment's shared courtyard would have sufficiently numbed my aching feet after class, but there was no time for hypothermia to set in. Sharon had invited Markus and the girls and me to a cosy little establishment that featured spontaneous live flamenco, courtesy of whomever was in the vicinity at the time. When we arrived at the café, several local musicians had already taken over half of the tables and were in the midst of a public jam session. As guitars were passed around, each of the young men took turns to sing a few *letras*, or verses. Enraptured by their sincerity and musicality, we clapped along and shouted encouraging words of *jaleos*. Evie took the appreciation one step further and bought the men several rounds of drinks. The more *cervezas* they consumed, the less they sang but it still made for a great *atmósfera*.

'This stuff's got quite the kick to it, Stace!' Evie approved as she and Madelyn took another sip from my cask of *sangría* in the courtyard afterwards. After several samples of it myself, I misguidedly chose to attempt to repair a hole in my practice skirt using a needle and thread Simone had kindly lent me. With tipsy eyes and rebellious hands, it took me 18 attempts to thread the needle alone. Just as I was beginning to make progress, a loud knock at the front gate sent my needle flying and our collective hearts racing. Seconds later, we were kidnapped.

I watched helplessly from the backseat of the speeding car as it snaked its way through the streets of Jerez, hurtling us further and further towards the dusky pink horizon beyond the edge of town.

'Do you know where we're going, Evie?' I shouted over the abrasive din of the engine. A robust, indecipherable Spanish phrase tumbled out of the driver's mouth, followed by a full-bodied raucous laugh. Evie giggled along and grabbed the spare hand of the driver that had reached back to pat her affectionately on the leg. I turned to Madelyn for support, but she was too focused on trying to take photos of the whirring cityscape. Sighing, I leant my head back on the seat and surrendered. At least if I was going to be held hostage for the evening, I was amongst friends.

Introductions had been brief and vague up until that point, but I'd heard enough about Sebastian's gregarious Uncle Vicente to know he was a good man, albeit a very persuasive one. Evie had met him on a previous trip to Jerez when she and Sebastian had stayed at Vicente's apartment. Ever the family man, Sebastian's uncle doted on Evie as if she was his own and it wasn't long before an unbreakable bond was forged between the two.

Something by the roadside suddenly made Vicente point and he made a very cheeky-sounding comment to his friend in the passenger seat. I strained my neck to get a better look at his mysterious friend but, just like our destination, his profile and character eluded me. As we drove past yet another unknown source of bemusement, Vicente shouted again; his free hand hitting the steering wheel as his eyes twinkled mischievously in the rearview mirror. It wasn't long before his infectious throaty laugh had us all in stitches.

Vicente's two-door hatchback then came to a grinding halt outside a suburban bar. Two of Vicente's *amigos* – whom also happened to own the place – were waiting for us and, after an inundation of hugs and kisses, we were shown to the best table in the house where the identity of our elusive passenger was finally revealed. His name was Kafele and was one of Vicente's dearest friends – a charming Egyptian man who just so happened to own another of Vicente's favourite bars. Vicente had invited Kafele to translate for the girls and me in lieu of Sebastian, who had briefly returned to Seville.

There was no sense delaying the inevitable. 'Um, Vicente …' I began nervously as Kafele collected our drinks from the bar. 'Um … *yo no puedo comer trigo.*' There was a moment of uncertainty before Vicente sprang to life. '*No gluten? Sí, no gluten!! No se puede comer gluten!*' He slapped his hand down on the table and burst into laughter. I beamed back at the jolly teddy bear of a man, instantly wanting to adopt him as well.

No expense was spared in Vicente's quest to show the girls and me a good time and, for the following two hours, conversations and merriment flowed abundantly as we supped on a smorgasbord of sherry, red wine and succulent *tapas*. A group of older men from the table beside us happily joined in the festivities and even posed for photographs with us, laughing along with *cigarrillos* and *cervezas* in hand.

It was during that time that I unexpectedly and unequivocally fell – hard – for one of the country's national treasures – and it wasn't Vicente. It was the buttery, melt-in-your-mouth ecstasy that was *queso manchego*. It wasn't any old slice of generic dairy heaven. *Manchego* cheese was so exclusive, it could only be made from the milk of Manchega sheep from registered farms in the Castilla-La Mancha region of central Spain, where Don Quixote hailed from. The cheese had to be aged for a minimum of 60 days and only then, once the finished product met the requirements of the jovial-sounding Manchego Cheese Denomination of Origin Regulating Council, would it be stamped with a unique number confirming its authenticity. No wonder it tasted so darn good.

With full hearts and bellies we sped off in Vicente's car to continue the revelry at Kafele's bar where there was inevitably only one way for three sassy, sozzled *señoritas* to let their hair down and that was to dance up a frenzied storm to a CD of nonstop *sevillanas*. By the time Vicente dropped us home around midnight, we'd agreed to let him take us to his friend's *bodega* the following afternoon, where he promised inordinate amounts of free sherry would be waiting for us.

¡Olé!

21

EN LA DIANA DE LA TORMENTA
In the Bullseye of the Storm

With an abundance of *coreografía* to get through, Ángel launched straight into teaching some tricky new footwork from the *escobilla*. Naturally, that threw the old ducks into a tailspin and, when he could no longer stand their agonising plight, Ángel graciously took the time to personally tutor every single one of them. He even assisted Evie, who was so hungover from the previous evening's shenanigans she could barely retain water.

Uncle Vicente and his trusty hatchback were waiting for us back at the apartment after class. Embracing the nation's notion of *cuantos más, mejor* (the more, the merrier), Vicente insisted Markus join us for the afternoon's frivolities. Before we could find our seatbelts, we'd left Spanish suburbia in our blazing wake and were soon enveloped by cascading hills of luminous green grass, which brilliantly reflected the sun's joyful rays. There wasn't a whisper of a cloud to be found in the sapphire-blue sky. The countryside could not have been more charming, save for the odd spot of bull.

There's nothing Australians enjoyed more than gargantuan roadside objects. Whether it was the Big Prawn, the Big Banana, the Big Chook or the Big Avocado, there were very few Australians whose childhoods hadn't been immeasurably enriched by such enormous entities, or their adjoining gift shops. A decade earlier, when I'd been careening through the northern Spanish countryside on the whistle-stop tour of Europe, I'd felt an instant kinship with the giant, black bull-shaped billboards on the side of the road, even though I had no idea what they were advertising at the time. I should have guessed really – booze!

In the 1950s, a company by the name of The Osborne Group dreamt up a brilliant marketing campaign to promote one of its brandies by covering the Spanish countryside in colossal billboards in the shape of its company logo – the *Toro de Osborne*, or Osborne Bull. The bovines proved so popular, they remained in place for several decades until a little organisation known as the European Union decreed a ban on all roadside advertising of alcohol. The EU, however, had not taken into consideration how deeply the 14-metre-high creatures were ingrained into the national psyche and, before anyone could say cirrhosis of the liver, a local "Save the Bull" campaign was mounted.

After escalating public pressure and even the Supreme Court getting involved, the Ossy bull-boards were eventually allowed to remain on the grounds of aesthetic or cultural significance, so long as any advertising was completely blacked out. The familiar bull-shaped silhouette now adorns every kind of T-shirt and trinket imaginable.

To celebrate Ossy's 50th anniversary, 50 international celebrities – including Antonio Banderas and Dr. Phil McGraw – were invited to decorate significantly smaller versions of the bull, which were displayed all over the world before being auctioned off for charity. (What association American talk show host Dr. Phil had with Spain was anyone's guess, but I'm assuming it might have had something to do with his ability to cut through bull#@$%.)

Not everyone was on Team Ossy though. Two of Spain's most autonomous regions took great offence to the emblematic icon and soon came up with their own versions. In Basque, the Osborne Bulls were knocked down and replaced with *ovejas vascas*, or silhouettes of the local sheep breed. In Catalonia, giant-sized versions of the strong-willed *burro catalán*, or donkey, were erected to represent its fiercely independent community. Some creative soul even went so far as to produce donkey bumper stickers, including a naughty version of a donkey sticking it to a bull (which inadvertently helped to raise awareness of the dwindling population of local purebred donkeys that has astonishingly shrunk from 50,000 to 500 in recent years).

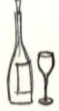

A long, bumpy dirt track escorted us to Vicente's friend's *bodega*, the happy position of which offered gloriously panoramic views of the incandescent valley below. The fact that Vicente's friend wasn't actually home was of no deterrent to our host, who immediately let himself in and began showing us around the place.

My liquid education in sherry had been woefully rustic up until I had arrived in Jerez. For most of my life, I'd believed there to be only two types of sherry – cooking or sweet – but apparently there were at least nine different varieties of pale and dark sherries, all of which derived from just three species of white grapes. (Originally there were over 100 different grape varieties, but a nasty bug invasion in the 1800s soon put a stop to that.)

My nightly jaunts around Jerez had introduced me to the luscious, warm mahogany tones of the *oloroso* and the sharp, shockingly deceptive nastiness of the straw-coloured *fino*. In my ignorant haze, I kept confusing the two and inevitably ended up ordering the latter; the flavour of which almost completely resembled licking a horse. It was no wonder that the type of white grape used to make such an arid excuse for paint-stripper was called the Palomino.

Around the time of my visit, Spain was producing over 70 million litres of sherry per annum and, just like the process of authenticating *queso manchego*, if the fortified wine wasn't created in the region known as the "Sherry Triangle of Spain", you couldn't call it sherry (unless you wanted to get sued, that was). What was more, the Spanish word for sherry was *jerez*, which would explain why the Festival de Jerez seemed to be equally about celebrating flamenco as it was about enjoying the local liquor.

Deep inside a cellar at his friend's *bodega*, Vicente offered us a taste of his most beloved sherry blend and proudly announced, through Markus's increasingly inebriated translation, that his friend had named that particular drop after him. With such an honour being bestowed upon the man, it would have been very rude of us not to taste a sample, or five.

Ever the attentive host, Vicente even remembered Evie's favourite sherry from her previous visit and graciously poured us all a serving of the richest, most heaven-sent, sweetest liquid amber ever to have danced across my palate. Unfortunately, hair of the dog wasn't working for Evie so I kindly polished off the rest of her glass.

In an adjacent storeroom, wooden vats the size of small cars were in the process of aging sherry; a process that could take up to 60 years to produce a concoction that could disappear in just 60 seconds. Talk about *dedicación*.

In yet another storeroom, Vicente showed us liquor in its innocent infancy before it had been seduced by the process of alcoholic fermentation. The aromas were the antithesis of delightful; matched only by a flavour best described as rotten cheese stored inside sweaty sneakers that had been left to fester in a dank wardrobe since the 1600s. It was, as they say, an acquired taste. We then slurred and swayed our way past a vinegar tank and saw where the grapes were crushed but even through molasses-coloured glasses, it was hard to ignore the dark shadows in our midst.

As we posed for photographs in the afternoon sun like one big drunk happy family, we spotted a curious, shy boxer dog lurking nearby. Although his eyes implored us to be friends, anytime anyone of us approached him, the poor little pooch would visibly cower and tremble. Then, as we stood gazing out over the property wall, I noticed several metal enclosures containing what appeared to be bird statues, positioned intermittently along the ledge. On closer inspection, I was sickened to see that five very-much-alive partridges were being held prisoner in individual cages so tiny, they couldn't even turn around inside them. The poor birds were doomed to stare vacantly out into the countryside, wearing their wooden coffins like a corset, with death being the only release from their cruel incarceration. How I desperately wanted to rescue them all!

Had I managed to do so, their cages wouldn't have stayed empty for long. I was witnessing firsthand the brutality of *silvestrismo*: an ancient practice that trapped and dramatically confined live songbirds in the appalling belief that they would sing more sweetly and/or attract other wild birds to the area. Here's an idea you scandalous *silvestrismo*-practising punks: why not leave the beautiful birds alone and just listen to them sing in the freaking trees where they belonged??

Mercifully, after centuries of practice – ¡¡centuries!! – songbird trapping was finally declared illegal by the EU in 2003 but, as with all sweeping, well-intentioned declarations, prosecution had yet to catch up with practice.

In addition to being forced to sing for their supper, the partridges were also unlucky enough to be one of the most hunted game birds around. Fun fact: according to the Spanish Ministry of Environment, around 4.2 MILLION birds were caught or killed in the country EVERY YEAR. Frankly, I was surprised there was any wildlife left at all. The poor little partridges were most likely being fattened up for the dinner table and/or being used to recruit their cousins to a similar culinary demise. Any way you looked at it, fried finch was not my idea of a good time and, as we left the property, I slid into a solemn despair, silently hoping there would be no more *confrontaciones culturales* in store.

A leisurely afternoon at the clifftop town of Arcos de la Frontera offered the perfect reprieve. Balanced on top of a craggy summit, reached by a labyrinth of steep and slender laneways, Arcos was one of Andalucía's most famed *pueblos blancos*, or white villages.

Vicente managed to score the last car park outside the pinnacle's impressive 13th-century gothic cathedral, before he eagerly ushered us inside a grandiose building sprawled majestically atop a steep rocky outcrop. Plush furnishings and lavish old-world charm infused the interiors set against the backdrop of a billion-dollar view. I couldn't work out what was more extravagant – the sumptuous surrounds or the eccentric-sounding English menu translations. Had I been even remotely hungry and excessively wealthy, I would have treated myself to a platter of "muffled shrimp", followed by a seductive serving of "buns of cod". A simple cup of tea won out in the end.

In such decadent opulence, it was a shame the wait staff hadn't got the memo that it was a bit of a classy joint. As several over-the-top, frilly-skirted hostesses who looked like they'd come straight from Oktoberfest flitted past our table, at least I knew where all of Ángel's biddies went on their afternoons off.

After high tea, we spilled out onto the hotel's open-air terrace. Approaching grey storm clouds merely heightened the contrasting colours of the olive orchards and the rich, red soil of the lush Guadalete Valley below.

'Hey check this out, guys!' Madelyn called us over to the outdoor dining area. Every tabletop was decorated with beautiful hand-painted tile mosaics depicting male and female flamenco dancers, with each image representing a specific flamenco *palo*. Every tile was exquisitely unique and I was pretty sure if they weren't superglued to the tables, Madelyn would have taken them home with her.

As the sparkly mountain air invigorated our senses, we became smitten with silence as eagles soared grandly overhead. The tranquility was temporary, however, when an earth-shatteringly shrill brass band started up in the cathedral next door, instantly blasting us into oblivion.

'*Pata negra!*' Vicente called out from the driver's window as we passed a rather curvaceous woman on our descent. '*Pata negra!*' Vicente gleefully shouted again, his calloused hands slapping the steering wheel as we drove past yet another lady blessed in the curve department. For the uninitiated, *pata negra* is a highly sought-after ham sourced exclusively from black Iberian pigs (*pata negra* means black hoof); an overindulgence of which could lead to an old man in his hatchback yelling, '*Pata negra!*' at you as you went about your daily business. It was a good day not to be a pedestrian.

It was truly an impressive feat. Whilst keeping an eye on passing foot traffic, Vicente managed to navigate his old rust bucket down alleyways so constricted, they accommodated only one car and one voluptuous woman at a time. When faced with oncoming traffic and nowhere to safely pull over, Vicente would channel his inner Italian and beep the horn, yelling and gesticulating wildly out of the window until the crisis was averted. As soon as the coast was clear, he was back yelling, '*Pata negra!*' again.

'Where are we now? Um … *dónde aqui?*' I asked as we pulled up beside a rustic patch of countryside.

'*Mi campo!*' Vicente grinned from ear to ear.

'*Campo?* Are we at some kind of camping ground now?' I asked the others.

'Nah, Stace, this is where Vicente and his mates grow all their veggies,' Evie explained.

'Ooh, I love community gardens,' I enthused. 'Free food!'

'*Burrrrrp*,' responded Evie in anticipation, her freckles sparkling in the afternoon sun.

The flourishing farm was a true testament to Vicente's devotion. He was so dedicated to his particular patch of earth, he awoke early every single morning to gently tend to each crop resulting in onions, tomatoes, potatoes and lettuces bursting with vitality and verve. Over in the orchard, plump juicy oranges dangled tantalisingly above us and, before you could say *jugo de naranja*, Vicente climbed a step ladder and enthusiastically shook one of the trees, causing a bounty of sweet nectar to rain down upon us.

Apparently *campos* weren't just about growing food. They were also a fabulous location for throwing parties. Before our visit, Vicente's plot had been transformed into a magical garden wonderland, complete with lanterns and homemade *paella* cooked traditionally in one of the giant pans stored in the on-site shed.

Just before dusk, Vicente invited us back for a drink at his sprawling apartment complex. With a large, communal swimming pool and schmancy tennis courts, it felt like much more of a resort than a block of units. No wonder Sebastian was a regular visitor.

As we entered Vicente's spacious sanctuary, it instantly felt like home and, for the next couple of hours, our gracious host lovingly plied us all with sherry, wine, breadsticks and *chorizo*. He then whipped up a batch of homemade fried octopus for us to enjoy – all while painstakingly showing me which foods were safe from gluten.

No visit to Vicente's quarters would ever be complete, however, without a look inside his infamous freezer. For years I had heard tall tales about its contents and, for the record, let me assure you it is all true. Hidden behind ubiquitous packets of frozen peas and tubs of ice cream was an assortment of entirely snap-frozen whole birds and rabbits with all of their feathers and fur intact. My Year of Eating Meat was fast dwindling down to just a month.

After that evening's Teatro spectacular starring the inimitable María Pagés, we were invited to rejoin Vicente at some kind of renowned meat restaurant for a post-show drink. The thought of even more carnivorous calamities made me want to curl up in the foetal position and munch on my body weight in spinach, so I graciously declined.

On my way back to the apartment, in an adjacent alleyway off the main drag, I spied a crowd of shifty-looking men holding white horseshoe-shaped toilet lids – all of whom looked extremely guilty and tried to hide when they saw me. Either I had just stumbled across the secretive lair of the local Toilet Seat Troubadours, or the display was simply a community service reminder to use less toilet paper. Sadly, by then, I was too tired to care.

22

ARRANQUE
Spontaneous Outbursts of Emotion

There was always one. As Ángel's workshop progressed, it became increasingly obvious that one of his petite older students possessed not only the muscular strength of a feather but also the attention span of a gnat. The woman turned up late to class every day (well, later than me), could not get through the warm-ups without taking a break and, as soon as the choreography became even remotely demanding, she would potter around and check her phone for messages. She was, for all intents and purposes, a complete and utter dingdot of the highest distraction. The *prestigio* of being in the same room as Ángel's *anatomía* for an entire week was clearly not enough for some.

As Ángel started the students on a section of fast and furious new footwork, Señora Dingdot went around and shut all of the studio windows. She then put her street clothes back on over her dance gear, left the room, sauntered back in and then deliberated about whether to take her flamenco shoes off or not. Just as we were collectively ready to hurl our water bottles at her, Ángel swooped in and encouraged her to stay to at least observe the class. She had, after all, paid a fortune to be there.

Not only did she take Ángel's advice and plonk down on a chair in the corner, Señora Dingdot then began filming the poor man. Recording flamenco superstars in class was an unpardonable sin, punishable by a diet of overpowering olives for all eternity. If any filming *was* allowed, it was usually of the students only. Any brief digital glimpses of your teacher's bicep – or buttock – in the side of frame should only ever be purely *accidental*.

Complicated rhythms were coming thick and fast and as Ángel patiently sang the different beats and patterns out aloud to us, we collectively hung off his every syllable, willing our brains and bodies to absorb every nuance. Everyone, that was, except Señora Dingdot who had crossed to the other side of the studio and struck up a lively, one-sided conversation with the class *cantaor*. When dialogue was not forthcoming, she went back to her seat and resumed filming until she was reprimanded by the singer himself who told her if she must record, it should only be of Ángel's feet. If it had been up to me, I would have confiscated her camera (for "research purposes") and kicked her out of class for good.

A slice of *tortilla y mayonesa y ensalada* at one of my new favourite cafés afterwards did nothing to quell my crankiness. Neither did lying angrily in bed for a couple of hours, begging for respite from the relentless construction noise – and flamenco footwork – next door. Only a bottle of sherry

Vicente "gifted" the girls and me from his friend's *bodega* managed to put things into perspective.

Javier Barón was the guest artist at the Teatro with a show entitled *Dos Voces para un Baile* or "Two Voices for a Dance". Belying his middle-aged years, Javier was a master of *compás* and performed seamless transitions alongside lightning-fast footwork. Unfortunately, I couldn't connect to any of Javier's energetic choreographies due to Loud Palmas Lady beside me. She had become so infuriatingly deafening, I'd finally resorted to putting an earplug in my left ear but that meant every time I leant back to talk to Simone in between numbers, I was either whispering or screaming at her. Two voices, indeed.

As brilliant as such polished, dynamic shows at the Teatro were, they were only ever a snippet of the flamenco on offer at the festival. Some of the more raw, spontaneous offerings were found in the *peñas*, or flamenco clubs, afterwards. Unlike touristy *tablaos*, *peñas* were like secret little folk societies, tucked away in the back streets of town, run by purists who preferred to focus on the product rather than the packaging. Costumes and staging were kept to an absolute minimum to ensure flamenco was expressed in its simplest, most immediate form. Better still, drinks were dirt cheap and there was barely an entrance fee. The only hitch was *peñas* never opened until very, VERY late.

'You joining us, mate?' Evie asked as we spilled out into the foyer after Javier's show.

'When does it start again?' I glanced at my watch.

'One o'clock. Come on, Stace. You don't want to miss out on this!'

I offered my friend a weary smile. 'I really need to get some sleep. Sorry, Evie.' I hugged her goodnight. 'I'll definitely go to the next one with you though.'

I was evidently, and unmistakably, out of my mind. Within moments of resting my head on the pillow, the landlords decided to crank up their television and watch a late-night movie at the extreme end of the decibel spectrum. By 2:30 a.m., when my friends had returned from the *peña*, I still hadn't slept a wink.

Finally, just as I was drifting off around 4 a.m., one of the landlords' windows unlatched itself and broke into a frenzied *compás*, banging out an unidentifiable rhythm above my head.

'#@$%!' I cursed as I gathered up the blankets and moved to the couch. Right on cue, the landlords got their second wind and burst into a *fin de fiesta* directly above my lounge room, forcing me to return to bed. A precious few hours later, the sweet dulcet din of hammering stabbed at all my senses.

And people wondered why I wasn't a morning person.

23

GANCHO
Getting Hooked

Spanish cable television was a remarkable institution. The girls' television set was a mere 12 metres away from mine yet offered a plethora more channels. As a result, Evie and Madelyn had become hooked on a station that played nonstop Italian music videos, whilst I'd become enamoured with a Spanish-dubbed American soap opera. I had no idea what the name of the show was, nor the plot, but everyone looked so gosh-darned happy and attractive all the time, I was unable to switch it off.

From what I could ascertain, the saccharine, overtly moralistic storylines seemed to revolve around a quirky blonde woman, her Golden Retriever, her female African American best friend (the blonde's, not the dog's), and some gratuitously clichéd old guy that no one really cared about but seemingly only tolerated because he was obscenely rich. The best character was Blondie's love interest; a delicious stud muffin of a man who worked as either a lawyer, a vet, a doctor or a cleaner. Naturally, both Blondie and Multi-Tasking Man were oblivious to the blazing sexual chemistry between them, but gosh darn it if her dog didn't do ridiculously cute things to try and bring them together every episode. It was so *adictivo*, I almost forgot about Ángel.

Of all the injuries you could sustain doing flamenco, there was one that was always best avoided. During the lesson, when most of Ángel's students were intently focused on incorporating upper bodywork into the choreography, a young Chinese woman suddenly yelped out in pain and crumpled to the floor. The poor girl had accidentally slammed the heel of one shoe down hard on the toes of the other; a mistake you only ever made once. Within seconds, Ángel was by her side and sat her on his bended knee as he removed her shoe and tenderly inspected her foot for damage. Next, an icepack was summoned and a chair provided so that the injured student could watch the rest of the class in comfort (well away from Señora Dingdot). What a man.

Later, when Ángel wandered throughout the studio to check on the students' progress, he stopped by a diminutive older Japanese lady and staged a mock bullfight with her. Caught completely unawares, she giggled and played along like a schoolgirl. The heartwarming spectacle concluded with Ángel wrapping his arms around her and planting a mischievous kiss on her forehead.

¡¿Honestly, was it *that* hard to replicate such men in Australia?!

A charming, open-air patio bar provided a gorgeous backdrop for Evie, Sharon and me to indulge in a drink after class. Just as I was tucking into some *patatas y chorizo*, Evie – who'd been scrambling around in her handbag – happened upon one of her credit cards and let out a yelp of joy. It wasn't the card itself that was so thrilling, but what remained on it from her recent trip to London – small clumps of floury-looking particles that she immediately scooped up and rubbed across her teeth.

Jerez wasn't the only city seeing its fair share of white powder. Snow had started falling in Madrid and the icy winds were already making their presence felt down south. To escape the blustery chill, Madelyn and I invited Evie and Markus to the Moorish tea house where, snuggled amongst huge satin cushions, we sipped on steaming, hot vanilla *té* topped with rich, creamy *leche*. Once Evie discovered that the *tetería* also served shisha, she immediately ordered one of the fruity flavours for us to try.

Never having heard of shisha before (I was from the country after all), I wasn't in the mood for getting high on some massive Turkish bong and declined the grape-scented hookah as it was passed around. Madelyn gave it a red-hot go but it was Markus and Evie – channelling their inner

Cheshire cats – who had the blowing of smoke curls down to a fine art.

'To hell with it,' I thought as it was offered the second time around. I vainly tried to follow the instructions of drawing just a little of the vapours into my mouth, before I ended up gasping and spluttering when most of it ended up in my lungs. The bitter tobacco aftertaste ensured I never went back for more.

When we exited the hookah house, I caught sight of a flyer taped to a nearby streetlamp and almost fell over when I read what it was advertising. Farruquito, one of THE most famous and insanely talented male flamenco dancers of all time, was holding a dance workshop in Jerez the following week.

To put it lightly, Farruquito was a freaking legend. With his family revered as one of the most famous flamenco dynasties ever, Farruquito was literally born into *compás*. Following his Broadway debut at the age of five, he captured the world's attention as the standout performer in Carlos Saura's film *Flamenco*, where the 12-year-old prodigy danced an explosive *soleá* with his grandfather, El Farruco (who was considered one of the best flamenco dancers of *his* generation). Farruquito offering a dance workshop was like Daniel Day-Lewis giving acting lessons.

There was only one catch: as Farruquito's workshop wasn't an official part of the festival, the €160 price tag would not include nightly entry to the Teatro shows. I agonised over whether I could manage Farruquito's classes as well as the non-refundable workshop Madelyn and I had booked to do the following week, but the *medio* level of the *mantón* workshop would no doubt demand even more stamina and concentration than Ángel's beginner's workshop. Energy-wise, I knew I wouldn't be able to pull it off, let alone pay for it.

Only one pursuit could distract me from the growing haze of despondency that lurked within. As my friends returned to their respective apartments for a *siesta*, I sidled up to the nearest tourist office.

'*Perdón. Dónde está El Corte Inglés?*'

The department store was only supposed to be a 20-minute walk away from the centre of town. Technically, I could have caught a bus but finding the correct stop, let alone the right bus, before making sure I had enough change for a ticket would have taken me the rest of the week. As I pounded the pavement, the crisp autumn sunshine warmed my mood considerably and diffused the chill off the gusty wind that threatened to knock me over at every step.

After a good 20-minute trek, there were still no signs of the tourist mecca. Every approaching intersection revealed yet another stretch of suburbia, sparse empty parklands and the occasional tobacconist. Only after another 20 minutes of power-walking did the shopping Shangri-La finally appear.

Once inside its polished marble interiors, my skin was instantly blasted with air-conditioning, elevator music offended my ears and sharp, fluorescent lighting burned my retinas. There was no doubt about it: I was home. I was so excited to have finally found El Corte Inglés, I rushed straight to the restroom and made immediate use of its abundant free toilet paper.

Over in ladieswear, my pulse quickened to find an entire rack of lush, silky *mantones* hand-stitched with the most exquisite embroidery – until I discovered the prices ranged from the most basic €140 model to a top-of-the-range silk design at €2,995 – almost $5,000 AUD for a freaking scarf!! I gingerly returned the *mantones* to their hangers, cringed at a selection of brash *sevillana* dresses so loud that even a hearing-impaired person would take offence to, then decided to splurge on the one thing that was truly missing in my life: writing paper.

With the popularity of the maths and spelling show *Cifras y Letras,* one would assume reading and writing would be customary staples in such an educated, intelligent society. It was rather strange then that the only writing paper available was either bound in expensive leather covers or masquerading as tiled graph paper from the third grade. It made no sense, particularly as it was well and truly before people's lives had become digitally diarised. After endless and earnest aisle hopping, even the toilet paper began to look good.

El Corte Inglés may not have cared for writing apparatus, but the department store sure liked to look after your waistline. In the grocery department, I stumbled across an entire AISLE of gluten-free goodies. It was more allergy-friendly food than I'd seen in my entire life, combined. Forget Ángel's sizzling hot buns, those room temperature hamburger buns were worth the trek alone. In the end (and mostly because I didn't feel like lugging a huge bag of carbs across Jerez), I settled upon a modest selection of gluten-free bread rolls, croissants and crackers.

After my inspirational mini-shopping spree, I resolved to find a more reasonably priced *mantón* at one of the local stores in town. Sure enough, two minutes before closing time in the most expensive-looking shop in all of Jerez, I purchased my first ever *mantón* – a shiny, jet-black number embossed with luminous red flowers for the bargain price of €120.

'What's the name of tonight's show?' I asked Simone as we took our seats in the theatre.

'*De Entre La Luna y Los Hombres* which means "Between the Moon and Men",' she replied.

I excitedly settled into my seat, anticipating a smorgasbord of hotties in various states of undress. Instead, the production turned out to be all about women – or more specifically – up-and-coming dancer Fuensanta la Moneta. Fuensanta was a beautiful dancer with a clean, neat dancing style, which she highlighted by wearing either a white nightie or cotton sheet for most of the performance. She even became her own backup dancer at one point, courtesy of videos projected onto long, white hanging drapes through which I managed to spy the odd musician every now and then.

The standout piece by far, though, was when Fuensanta glided onto the stage in a stunning red *bata de cola*. Both her rich, long velvety dress and the powerful *seguirya* she performed were truly triumphant. The only letdown was her sound and lighting team who must have been on *siesta*. When Fuensanta was bowing for the second curtain call of the evening, all of the house lights suddenly blazed on, leaving the poor woman trapped like a deer in headlights and audience members stunned as to whether to continue their standing ovation or bugger off to the bar. Fortunately, they found a way to do both.

24

UN DÍA DEL DESPLANTE
A Climactic Day

It was impossible to emotionally prepare for the last ever lesson with Ángel. It had taken years to turn my flamenco dreams into reality and the precious week with him was sadly almost over. Wisely, instead of cramming our minds and bodies with even more choreography, Ángel spent the final couple of hours getting us to practise the dance over and over again, teaching only a small *remate* to finish it off. Every time we ran the choreography from the beginning, half of the students would run off and grab their cameras to film the other half dancing. For some reason, Sharon decided to exclusively film *me* doing the entire dance. When I watched the video back, I couldn't see a scrap of footwork, only my wiggly, red-skirted butt taking up most of the frame. Barbara, an older American lady from class, liked the video so much she asked for a copy. In hindsight, I should have charged a cheeky commission.

The most delightful moments, however, were when Ángel jumped in and danced the entire *martinete* alongside us, which prompted one of the more respectful students to remind everyone not to film our much-loved teacher. Instead of nodding in agreement, Ángel shrugged his shoulders. '*Por qué no?*' he asked. 'Why? Eet eez okay if you film me. I don't mind.'

The students and I glanced at each another like stunned mullets. Had that meant for the past week we could have been extensively recording Ángel from every possible angle for our own private collection – I mean revision?! In the end, Señora Dingdot was the only one who managed to completely capture our cherubic idol on celluloid and, conveniently, she and her camera were nowhere to be found.

Collective fantasies of abducting Ángel after class to join us for celebratory drinks and *tapas* (and fight over who would sit next to him – or on his lap) came to an abrupt halt when his wife and daughters arrived to watch the final run-throughs.

It took me years before I realised the incredibly gorgeous lead female performer in Paco Peña's shows was also Ángel's wife – a divine dancer who effortlessly radiated grace, poise and a dynamic inner strength. Onstage, her long, languid backbends would put a chiropractor out of business and what she couldn't do with a castanet wasn't worth knowing. It was always a joy to watch such a *guapa* in action, I just wasn't prepared for her to return the favour, so when she arrived to watch the final moments of the workshop, I hid on the opposite side of the room. Ángel's eldest daughter, who bore a striking resemblance to her beautiful father, also chose to stay in the background. It didn't take a *genio* to figure out why.

'*Papi!*'

Upon spying her father, Ángel's youngest daughter let out a shriek of joy; her charming little baby doll dress upstaged only by her petite pink-and-white flamenco shoes. As we rehearsed the dance, the little *angelita* and her curly mop of raven ringlets bounced up and down as she tried to copy the choreography, before doing *palmas* for us – perfectly in time, I might add.

For the very last run-through, Ángel encouraged everyone to put down their cameras and dance one last time together.

'*Todos!* Please, we must all dance ze final dance *juntos. Eso es.*'

It was a beautiful sight. Young and old, German biddies, Aussie *chicas* and everyone in between threw down their recording devices and flung their last reserves of energy and passion into the *martinete*. When it was over, Ángel gave everyone a huge round of applause; his beaming smile and twinkling eyes conveying his immense pride at our progress.

As was custom for participants of the festival, we were each then to receive a Certificate of Attendance to prove we had indeed spent almost 13 hours of our lives with His Heavenly Hotness. One by one, Ángel read out each student's name to enthusiastic acclaim – and more importantly – hugs, kisses and a photograph with the man himself. My heart was pounding like a *rumba* as I watched Sharon, Markus and Evie collect their awards.

After an awkward pause and furrowing of Ángel's brow, I knew I was next.

'Eh-Stacey ... Mm ... Eh-bish-ah.'

Immediately, I stepped forward to accept Ángel's *abrazos y besos*, before I sweatily collected my certificate from his eldest daughter. As Ángel and I posed for photographs, I braved a lame joke about how famous we must have been with all of the paparazzi around us. To emphasise my point, I struck a pose like a conceited film star. *Click*. That was how the first photo turned out. Thankfully, Sharon asked us to pose again and, for the next shot, my face took on the dimensions of an overly eager sociopath – mementos I would treasure forever.

By the time the last of the German biddies had received their certificates, Ángel announced one more student would be getting an award, prompting everyone to look around for Señora Dingdot. 'Ze last person eez ...' Ángel then read out the name of his eldest daughter, who instantly broke into a huge toothy grin and lost herself in her daddy's embrace. There wasn't an unaffected ovary in the room.

After class, I noticed Ángel's wife sitting by herself in the corridor outside. My opening line of '*Habla inglés?*' went down a clunker when she replied, '*No*'. I somehow managed to ask her in impudent Spanish if she, herself, was also a teacher but again she rigorously shook her head. Thankfully, the much-more-fluent Sharon then appeared and I implored her to tell Ángel's wife what an exquisite and elegant dancer she was. The *bailaora* smiled graciously at the compliment, but I couldn't help but notice her eyes were tinged with a little fatigue. It was no wonder. Being married to the sexiest man in Europe would be enough to wear anyone out.

To celebrate our last afternoon together before Sharon and Evie flew the coop, we unanimously agreed to meet for one last soirée at the flamenco café. Several of the other students had decided to join us, but with a very different motivation in mind. Ángel just so happened to be at the very same café being interviewed by a Danish student for her local newspaper. I kicked myself for not having come up with the same idea. I could have cross-examined Ángel for *The Cuddly Chronicles* or *The Gluten-free Gazette*. As I snuck a look into the adjoining room, a man who I assumed to be Felipe, Ángel's manager – who I'd spoken to on the phone from Australia – was sitting alongside Ángel and his family. All throughout the interview the students and I sat in silence, unabashedly trying to eavesdrop on the multilingual exchange.

Once the formalities were over, however, it was time to party and Ángel's youngest daughter led the charge by launching off her mother's lap and straight into some very impressive footwork on the café's floorboards. She was then hoisted high onto a table where she improvised a delightful little *bulería*. As the rhythm gained momentum so, too, did her family's shouts of *jaleos* and *palmas* until, on the very count of 10, the little girl leapt into her daddy's waiting arms, squealing with laughter. With every customer's doting eyes upon her, she repeated the performance to rapturous applause.

(Had I been a few kilos lighter and 30 years younger, I might have had a go myself.)

My very last Spanish glimpse of Ángel was with a big, beautiful grin on his face, enjoying precious time with his beloved family, before he no doubt had to jump on a plane and teach another workshop at some far-flung destination. I lived in eternal hope that that somewhere would one day include Australia.

Isabel Bayón was debuting her first solo festival show at the Teatro entitled *Tórtola Valencia,* based on 19th-century flamenco performer and visionary Carmen Tórtola Valencia – an early modern dancer who often danced without any shoes on. Sadly, however, not even artistic innovation could save Carmen from being jailed at the end of the Spanish Civil War due to her political leanings and homosexuality.

As she glided out onto the stage, Isabel looked stunning in a lavish, Egyptian-style dress with her hair in an immaculate 1940s up-do. As she danced ever so elegantly, classic black-and-white film images played in the background. Fortunately, there were also plenty of opportunities for her cheeky persona to shine through and, just when audience members thought they'd seen every trick in the book, Isabel danced with a fan in both hands.

It wasn't possible for the show to get any better until a lone male singer, Miguel Poveda, took to the stage. Such was the power and intensity of his vocals, he brought the house down on his very first note. After performing a tender dance solo to Miguel's rich melodies, Isabel had another surprise up her sleeve (and it wasn't a castanet).

Matilde Coral, one of the greatest living matriarchs of flamenco – and Isabel's former teacher, waltzed out onto the stage and struck a pose. For a mature lady of 74 years, she still had it and although her movements were minute, the intention in which she executed them was immense. Matilde was regarded as the sole custodian of the Seville School of Dance: a classical dance style she had passionately promoted and performed for the better part of 50 years. What set the Seville style apart from other regional approaches was its focus on the upper body, positioning of the head, movement of the hips and arching of the shoulders – in stark contrast to the crazy muppet, anything goes-style of agitated flamenco to which I usually subscribed.

By the end of the performance, Isabel wasn't the only one with tears in her eyes. Matilde had well and truly stolen the show. Audience members were so astonished to witness such an unexpected guest star in action, they took a moment to collect themselves. Once consciousness was regained, the entire auditorium erupted into a thunderous standing ovation.

The gang and I were in great spirits at the bar afterwards – thanks to numerous liquid spirits – before the room suddenly fell silent. Isabel and Matilde had chosen our favourite little haunt for their official afterparty. We were so honoured to be in their presence, we became reverentially mute, including the normally chatty Vicente. I would have loved to offer both ladies my heartfelt congratulations on their incredible show, but I didn't have the *cojones*. (Besides, if Isabel had recognised me, she might have made me dance for Matilde so she, too, could look at me in confounded bewilderment.)

'I'm gonna miss you, mate.' Evie hugged me fiercely. 'Make sure you enjoy the rest of your time here, okay? Get to a *peña*, soak up all the flamenco you can and I'll see you when you get back to Brissie!'

'See you, Evie. It's not going to be the same without you, or your burps.' I giggled and squeezed her goodbye. 'Have a safe trip back!'

The only positive thing that came from Evie's departure was that I inherited the rest of her sherry.

¡Salud!

25

DESCARGA
Discharge of Electricity

I awoke with *la influenza española*.

But there was no time to be sick. Madelyn and I had hatched a plan to escape to Cádiz for the day and although we were too late to see Carnaval, the lure of finally being able to see the ocean was enticement enough. At my alarm clock's behest, I rolled my aching body out of bed and dragged myself out into the communal courtyard. I was just about to knock on Madelyn's door when she poked her sleepy head out and motioned for me to be quiet. I was confused. Hadn't Evie already departed earlier that morning? Madelyn refused to utter a word until we were safely within the confines of my abode.

'What a night!' Madelyn exclaimed, flopping onto the couch.

'What happened? Why do we have to be so quiet?' I insisted.

'Seb's asleep in my room.'

'Excuse me?!'

'Ssshhh,' she whispered then threw her arms up in exasperation. 'Not that he'd probably hear us, the way he bloody snores.'

'Mads! What's going on?!'

'Right, well after you left the bar last night, we went to that good old meat restaurant. When Vicente called it a night, the rest of us kicked onto a couple of *peñas* and saw some shows. Hang on.' Madelyn paused. 'Can I get some water please?'

'Sure thing,' I said, pouring her a glass as quickly as the plumbing would allow.

'Ah thanks.' She sipped graciously. 'The *peñas* were awesome by the way, Stace! So many students there and the shows were incredible. You would have loved it.'

I nodded, wrapping the 200 or so layers I was wearing tighter around me.

'Then we went to a bar down the road and saw a few of the *peña* performers. Seb tried talking to some of them, but they were off their nut on something apparently. Anyway, by then I'd had enough so I came back and crashed out around 3:30 a.m., but because Vicente had long gone, Seb needed somewhere to stay so Evie offered him our joint. About an hour later, Evie and Seb decided to have a big fry-up in the kitchen.'

'Then what happened?' I prodded.

'They eventually went to bed and because there was nowhere else to sleep, Seb crashed on the couch.'

'Fair enough.'

'Once Seb passed out, he started snoring like a bush pig on heat.' Madelyn continued. 'Shortly after, Evie dropped by Markus's apartment and apparently had a bit of a snog fest before she left to catch the early train, after which time Seb ended up sleeping in her bed.'

'Hang on. What?! Evie got with Markus?!'

'Sounds like it.'

'And then Seb ended up in Evie's bed?'

'After she'd gone, yeah.'

I paused to let it all sink in.

'Nothing happened between you guys too, did it?' I asked, my eyes wide as saucers.

'God no, Stace! It's Seb!'

A crimson blush began to creep across my face. Back in Brisbane, at the height of our flamenco education, Sebastian had invited me over to his place to watch flamenco videos one evening. It wasn't the first time we'd hung out alone but for some reason – most likely due to consuming copious amounts of alcohol – Sebastian started telling me how beautiful I was. Before I could catch my breath, he started kissing me. Hold the phone?! Sebastian was kissing me?! Having never thought of him that way before (well, not consciously anyway), I was plunged into intoxicated shock. For most of the time I'd known him, Sebastian had been in a long-term relationship but since that had ended, he'd been footloose and fancy-free.

Only when I started kissing Sebastian back did it all suddenly make sense. We were two passionate people, fuelled by our desire for flamenco. It was a match made in heaven!

Although it stayed rather G-rated, I couldn't help but notice our chemistry was off the charts and, in my dating naiveté, believed it could have been the start of something special. Sadly, it was not to be. Shortly afterwards, Sebastian fell into a long-term relationship with another dancer from class.

Madelyn rested her head on the couch. 'I'm stuffed, Stace.'

'Should we take a rain check on Cádiz then?'

'Nope, give me an hour. I'll be good to go.' She was such a trooper.

By the time she was ready, Madelyn was hankering for a caffeine boost but, being a Sunday, there weren't a lot of options available. Convinced she could at least find someone selling *churros* somewhere, Madelyn combed the streets of Jerez, whilst I ducked into a nearby internet café to book our tickets to Cádiz.

¡¡#@$%!!

According to the online timetable, the next train wasn't until 3:15 p.m. and, by the time it arrived, there would've been very little daylight left to explore the coastal city. With our brand new dance workshop starting the following day, our dreams of Cádiz would sadly have to remain just that. Disheartened, Madelyn went back to bed and, just as she fell asleep, Sebastian woke up.

'Stace! You missed a great night last night.' He greeted me with a dishevelled hug.

'So I hear,' I said as unwistfully as I could.

'What are you doing now? Wanna grab a bite to eat?'

(For the record, I will always answer that question in the affirmative.)

'They have markets here?!' I exclaimed as we walked through the bustling square outside the Supermercado.

'Yep, every Sunday.' Sebastian guided me through a warehouse packed with fruit and vegetable stands. Together, we grabbed lunch from one of the nearby vendors and sat eating in silence; Sebastian in the throes of a hangover and me quashing any long-lost romantic regret with a plate of *patatas bravas*.

'*Aiiiiiiii.*'

A voice sang out across the plaza. I shot up from my stool and bolted outside. Standing around in a huddle were four elderly gentlemen; one of whom could no longer contain his grief.

'*Aiiiiiiii.*'

Immediately, his three mates began rapping their knuckles on the top of a wine barrel, offering him *compás*. It was a mesmerising illustration of *cante a golpe* – the purest form of flamenco you could encounter.

I pulled on Sebastian's jacket. 'They're singing flamenco, Seb! Right out in the open!'

'Yeah.' He shrugged. 'It's Spain.'

The fact that Madelyn was in a deep sleep when we returned to the apartment was of no impediment to Sebastian, who snuck in and "borrowed" her laptop so we could watch practical jokes being played on people until she woke up.

The outrageously talented and ultra-modern dancer Rocío Molina was the star performer at the Teatro that evening. Although only in her early twenties, Rocío had already been around flamenco long enough to have injected her own style and was considered one of the best new artists of her generation. Rocío was like a mini firecracker, lulling the audience into a fleeting sense of security before she suddenly exploded with very sharp, snappy choreography.

One of her backup dancers was a beguiling addition, especially when Rocío danced a very saucy duet with her (which made even more sense when I discovered the two were, in fact, an item). Rocío's show *Oro Viejo*, or "Old Gold", went on to win the Critics Award for the entire festival.

Had I been in charge, I would have bestowed a slightly different honour: that of Best Stage Names to the members of her band. The name of Rocío's singer was La Tremendita (or The Tremendous), and her two *palmeros* had the enviable nicknames of Eléctrico and Bobote – the latter of which loosely translated to a bit of a silly person. Nice.

Not everyone in the flamenco industry could run around calling themselves Fancy Feet or Lord of the Strings though. Unless you were assigned one as a child and spent the rest of your career trying to shake it off, you had to earn your *mote*, *apodo* or flamenco nickname.

Wisely, the late, great guitarist Francisco Sánchez Gómez claimed his stage name before anyone else could. With Paco being the abbreviation of Francisco, and Lucía being the name of his dearest mother, Paco de Lucía (aka Francisco from his Mother) chose well.

Singer José Monge Cruz had no chance of retaining his original moniker. Due to his fair complexion and lanky physique, José's uncle called him Camarón – or Shrimp – from the get-go, which then evolved into Camarón de la Isla, or Shrimp of the Island. Nowadays, San Fernando, where Camarón was born, is more like a peninsula, but Camarón de la Península doesn't have quite the same ring.

Other top flamenco nicknames over time have included: La Niña de los Peines (The Girl of the Combs), El Borrico de Jerez (The Donkey of Jerez) and El Mojama (The Salt-Cured Tuna). I so longed for a stage name of my own. I could be Pata Negra Aspirante (Wannabe Boombah), Chica Curvilínea del Pelo Corto (Curvy Girl of the Short Hair), or even Despreciador del Trigo (Wheat Scorner).

The options were endless.

26

GUAPAS Y GUAPOS
Hotties of Every Persuasion

She was the most beautiful doll I had ever seen. Her face was exotic, dark and beautiful; her expression serene. No matter the angle, her rich chocolatey eyes appeared to dance in the light. Resplendent ruffles cascaded down her turquoise bodice, culminating in a long, gilded *bata de cola* that flowed gracefully behind her. Nestled inside her jet-black bun was a small blue hair comb and wrapped around her delicate fingers were tiny black castanets.

Unless you counted an olive oil advertisement from the 1980s where a lady squished an olive under her shoe, I'd had zero concept of what flamenco was when my father gifted the doll to me as a young child. Had I known, I would have instantly given up lip-synching to Olivia Newton-John albums and thrown myself at flamenco's fiery feet for all eternity.

Little wonder then for the second week of the festival, I had desperately wanted to enrol in a *bata de cola* workshop so

I, too, could flounce around in a stunningly long dress like my beloved Spanish doll wore. *Bata de colas* (which literally meant coats or gowns with a tail) were the bridal gowns of the flamenco world – what each and every single female dancer (and quite possibly some of the men) aspired to own, if only the dresses weren't so exquisitely expensive. I would have been ecstatic just to stand and pose in one like a prima donna, but the whole idea was to actually *dance* in them.

If my former dressmakers thought sewing a basic flamenco dress was complicated, asking them to make a *bata* would have cemented their early retirement. It was such a precise art that, in addition to requiring truckloads of fabric and frills for both the inside and out, metres of wiring and boning had to be covertly sewn into the seams to produce the perfect weight. Too light, and the skirt would float and flip all over the place. Too heavy, and the dancer wouldn't even be able to stand up. Since I didn't own a *bata de cola*, and hadn't known I could have hired one at the festival until I arrived (¡#@$%!), I'd chosen the *mantón* workshop instead.

On our way to the first lesson, I convinced Madelyn to take a detour past the construction site beside our apartment so we could give Ruthlessly Hammering Man and his new friend, Relentlessly Drilling Man, stink-eye but once we saw how handsome they both were, they received only flirty smiles from us instead.

Our new studio for the week was high above the Teatro, with windows overlooking the bustling courtyard below. I hoped our new teacher would go easy on us in the first class, especially as I was still fighting off a cold. Fortunately, all doubts were quelled the moment I laid eyes on Blanca: a beautiful, immaculately groomed woman with kindness in her eyes and a genuine, welcoming smile. Elegant rings adorned her gracefully manicured fingers; her long chestnut hair was tied back neatly in a bun and her wonderfully maintained skin radiated wellbeing from every pore. If my Spanish doll had had a real life mother, Blanca would have been it.

Like all the flamenco greats, Blanca was born into dance and spent years honing her craft in the top Spanish *tablaos*, before gracing stages the world over from Tunisia to Taiwan. She'd had just about every prestigious award thrown at her and, at one point, was the EU Representative of Spanish Dance. Blanca was highly regarded for her flawless creativity, technical perfection and *puro* flamenco approach to the craft. However, if she was to be remembered for just one thing, it would be her most enduring masterpiece; the *palo* for which she was most famous – the *soleá con mantón* – the very dance Madelyn and I had booked to learn from the gracious goddess herself.

In soft-honeyed tones, Blanca summoned for the class to begin and every student immediately assembled into position – 23 experienced-looking dancers and two Australian girls nervously pawing at their shawls in awkward anticipation. In stark contrast to the demographic of Ángel's workshop, the average age of the attendees was about 30 and although there were some German ladies in attendance, thankfully they wouldn't be qualifying for biddy status for many years to come.

Madelyn and I positioned ourselves up the back alongside a Chrissie Amphlett look-alike who sported a punk hairdo and leg warmers. She lasted only the first lesson. As the singer and guitarist took their places, Blanca explained to her protégés about the intricacies of working with a *mantón* and the relationship we each had to develop with our shawls for everything to go smoothly. (The only reason Madelyn and I gleaned any of this was thanks to a young Dutch student who kindly translated for us.)

The next two hours unfolded like an initiation into a secret society. First, Blanca demonstrated how to grip a shawl. Finger placement was crucial. The most natural method of grabbing the material between the thumb and forefinger was considered unsightly and non-flamenco. The correct and covert technique, Blanca elucidated, was to slip your hand underneath the *mantón* and clasp the material between your fingers, like a hairdresser held hair to be trimmed. The biggest downfall with shawls, though, was that they could be slippery suckers and, unless you had sandpapered the inside edges of your fingers or bound them in Velcro, you always had to hang on for dear life.

Satisfied with the progress of the majority of the students, Blanca then demonstrated the opening steps of the *soleá*. We commenced by cocooning ourselves in our shawls until we resembled Spanish mummies. We then slowly extended our right arms out and unwrapped our shawls, circled them around our heads, before we unwrapped them and circled our arms around again. It was like the "Dance of the Seven Indecisive Veils". Next, we turned our bodies slowly in the direction of our unravelling *mantones* until they ended up behind our backs, before we wrapped them around our waists ready for more. It couldn't have been simpler, really.

Soleás were normally very heavy songs seeped in tragedy and despair, but the one we would be learning, Blanca explained, would be sweet and light – unlike our shawls. When half the class began repeatedly tripping over their tassels, Blanca kindly let us in on another secret: no matter what kind of knot you tied yourself into, you would always be able to get out of it. It was a great metaphor for life.

'See here, ladies. If the *mantón* gets tangled up in your feet, just turn around and keep spinning until it has unravelled. Like so.' She kindly demonstrated.

'Ooooooh,' we responded in grateful unison.

'If you drop your shawl, acknowledge it. Make it part of the performance. Dance around it until a suitable moment when you can pick it up.' I pushed away visions of interpretative dancing around my shawl like a mad woman at a hippie festival.

'However, the most important lesson I will ever teach you is this: you have to love your *mantón*.'

Madelyn and I stole a furtive glance at each other.

'You have to get to know your *mantón* inside and out, learn from it, embrace it, sleep with it – yes, ladies – sleep with it! And, most importantly, never ever get angry or frustrated at your *mantón*. Why? It is an extension of you and therefore as beautiful as you.'

She was like the Louise Hay of Flamenco. I could have listened to her for hours (via our Dutch translator) but we had a dance to learn. Blanca then allocated the next 10 minutes for us to get to know our shawls. Smoke was billowing out of my ears after only a couple of minutes of shooting the breeze with mine so, when no one was looking, I snuck into the changing rooms and scoffed down the rest of my gluten-free toast.

As hard as I tried, I couldn't concentrate for the rest of the lesson. Every time Blanca extolled the virtues of adoring our shawl, or showed us variations of the opening steps, a strange kind of wet sound followed by a booming male voice pervaded the studio. The frustrating thing was no one else seemed to notice. Either I was going mad or I was hearing festival noise from the marquees below.

Just then, raucous laughter reverberated around the room and I looked over in disbelief to see the class guitarist having a good old chinwag with the singer, whilst he stuffed lunch into his mouth directly in front of the microphone – none of which would have been a problem if the speaker levels weren't cranked up to *ridículo*. Then, towards the end of class, as I was finally getting the hang of a new step, the female singer's piercing shrieks rattled my bones so profoundly, I dropped my *mantón* in fright. After two hours, I was beginning to have no love left for anyone.

Madelyn and I took the scenic route back to our apartment and, down a previously unexplored side street, we happened upon the most exquisite flamenco store in Jerez where, in the decadent window display, was THE most beautiful *mantón* ever created: glossy and black, adorned in white floral embroidery and, in a twist no one saw coming, framed with the most delicate snow-white fringing imaginable. The *flecos*, or fringing, on every other shawl I'd seen up until then had always matched the material they were affixed to – which was usually basic black. This *mantón* was an absolute work of art and, at €120, was exactly the same price I'd paid for my hastily purchased black-and-red number a few days prior. My dwindling funds just couldn't take another hit. I was gutted.

For the second week of the festival, students were allocated a brand new seat in the Teatro and, with Loud Palmas Lady history (*¡Olé!*), my ears and I were curious to learn who our new neighbours would be.

'Is this my spot? Hey look! We're going to be buddies for the week.'

It was Barbara, the older American lady from Ángel's class, who was also the proud owner of my wiggly red butt video. I smiled politely, thinking of all the loud, brash comments I might have to endure. Fortunately, I could not have been more wrong. Barbara was tremendously intelligent, hip and funny. She was also so in love with flamenco, she attended the festival every year.

'Just you wait for tonight's show,' Barbara gushed. 'You're going to be blown away by the lineup.'

As the curtains parted, I was elated to finally witness one of flamenco's power couples in action: Andrés Peña and Pilar Ogalla. Not only did they both have wildly successful solo performing and teaching careers in their own right, they were also extremely good-looking. If the Joaquin Phoenix-like Andrés with his strong, powerful physique and devastatingly handsome chiselled face didn't do it for you; nor Pilar with her Jennifer Aniston good looks and tousled brunette hair, there was plenty more eye candy on offer in the Latino god and goddess department.

The four backup dancers alone looked like they'd stepped straight out of Spanish *Vogue*, and the band off the cover of *Rolling Stone*. The violinist was a smoky mop of dark curls and smouldering eyes, and the two guitarists resembled a longer-haired Javier Bardem and Spanish Hugh Grant respectively. Had I been on the board of the festival, I would have awarded the show The Highest Number of Hotties Ever Assembled on Stage. Period.

Just when I thought I had died and gone to flamenco heaven, a spotlight illuminated four singers who began belting their hearts out with all the ardour they could muster. I was unable to prise my eyes off the most striking of them all – a celestial being named David Palomar – whose sultry, powerful voice rendered him even more intoxicating.

'*Muy caliente*,' Barbara whispered.

'I've lost feeling in my limbs,' I concurred.

After some upbeat solos and electrifying duets, Andrés then knocked everyone's socks off with a *soleá*; the same style of dance we were learning from Blanca (minus the *mantón*).

With a bold, yet traditional style and raw, sexy masculinity oozing out of his every pore, Andrés was so mesmerising, I forgot to perve on the singer and made a mental note (*#3*) to learn from Andrés at least once in my life.

As was the custom for the final *fin de fiesta*, each performer was given the opportunity to wow the audience with their own improvisational prowess. (*Fin de fiestas* were typically when you'd see dancers sing, guitarists dance or singers play the guitar. The rules were: there were no rules, just so long as you stayed in *compás*.)

When a female backup dancer stepped forward to take her turn in the spotlight, I couldn't help but notice one of her male contemporaries very publicly adjusting himself around the groin area. 'Fondle yourself later, buddy,' I willed. 'We've paid good money (via a workshop) to see a professional show, not an amateur groper!' Whatever he was doing, he had to hurry, though, as it was his turn next.

When the male dancer took centre stage, it finally dawned on the audience what his problem was. The poor guy's fly had burst open and, with the zipper refusing to budge, he was forced into a split-second decision: would he try and cover up his tighty whities with a jacket and dance, or decline his solo and exit stage right? Enticingly, Fly Boy did neither and took complete ownership of the situation by proudly strutting around, drawing as much attention to his crotch with hand gestures and hip thrusts as he could. The audience roared its approval and, deservedly, he got the biggest applause of all. It was Barbara's favourite part of the show, too.

In keeping with the beefcake theme, the usual suspects and I adjourned to the good old meat restaurant after the performance. It was my first introduction to the animalistic institution, located beyond endless plazas and mazes of twisting cobblestoned streets (just for something different).

Once settled at the bar, I perused the notorious menu and was predictably troubled by the number of cooked creatures on offer so, in the name of scientific curiosity and kindness, I ordered a plate of *patatas bravas* that quickly put every other version I'd tried to shame. The potato squares were mouthwateringly crispy and smothered in a generous tomato sauce, with a big dollop of garlicky cream on top. It was so delicious, I suspected there may have been some hidden meat lurking in there.

Most inconveniently, there wasn't a single scrap of toilet paper to be found on the premises. I would have loved to have been a fly on the wall when Evie had thrown her weight around. One evening, she'd had enough of both wine and wiping her bottom with her hands and staged a showdown with the restaurant staff, demanding they provide her with some loo paper. When none was forthcoming, she stole some serviettes – a tradition I continued in her honour and absence. It took me a full two weeks before I realised I wasn't supposed to flush paper down the toilet at our favourite bar either. The fact that there were never any toilet rolls in the cubicle never seemed to register and, night after night, I warned queuing females that they were out of paper again, oblivious to the indecipherable signs on the back of the restroom door. I planned to send my apologies to the sanitation department of Jerez whenever I found some paper to write them on.

'How are you enjoying the festival so far?' Monique, a statuesque, blonde Canadian student, pulled up a stool beside me.

'It's awesome! I love seeing the shows and all the flamenco stars wandering around. I can't wait to come back!'

Monique smiled deferentially.

'Is this your first time here?' I asked.

'It's my first Festival de Jerez, but I've been in Seville for almost a year now,' she replied, taking a sip of her wine.

'Studying flamenco?' I was impressed. 'Don't you have to fly home every few months so you don't outstay your visa?' I knew that Australians were only allowed in the EU for three months at a time and had assumed the same applied to Canadians.

Monique shook her head. 'No. Well, technically yes, but while I'm here, I'm going to make the most of it.'

I looked at her in envious disbelief.

'I started flamenco in Toronto a couple of years ago and became obsessed. There, I could only do a couple of classes a week. Here, I'm doing a couple of classes a day.'

'But how do you support yourself? You're not allowed to work here, are you?' I enquired.

'Not officially. I babysit for cash and live in a share house with other students.'

'Geez the babysitting must pay well!'

Monique shrugged. 'It pays okay.'

'Classes are expensive to attend all year though. Surely you must struggle a bit?' I was like a dog with a bone.

She turned to look me square in the eye. 'My parents love me very much.'

'Ah,' I replied and went back to my *patatas bravas*.

27

EL PODER DEL PELO
The Power of Hair

Blanca could instantly tell we hadn't been sleeping with our shawls.

'Ladies, your *mantón* is your friend,' she explained. 'Your *mantón* is always right. It always falls elegantly and how it's meant to. It's up to you to work out how you can redeem yourself without looking like a complete and utter cowboy.' (*NB: not a direct translation.*)

'If your shawl coils around your feet, a graceful way out is to grab the *flecos* like so. These are the hands of the *mantón*. Gently turn the other way, keeping in time to the music and it will unfold for you. If your *mantón* gets caught in your hair or earrings, be patient and graceful, extracting yourself as attractively as possible.'

Blanca demonstrated each of the scenarios for us, always at one with her shawl. When we were ready to dance, she showed us the next sequence of steps, demonstrating a completely different version every time. If you hadn't picked up the steps in the first instance, and couldn't remember the second or third variations, you sure had your work cut out for you. I'd always assumed the whole idea of workshops was to learn a big chunk of choreography that would instantly become part of your performing repertoire but I was proved refreshingly wrong.

Some of the more advanced students managed to completely memorise, categorise and collate every example into one solid, impressive showcase but whenever Madelyn and I tried to imitate our teacher, we ended up duplicating a train wreck instead. Frustrated at some of her students' flailing attempts at improvisation, Blanca announced she would not be lowering the level of the class to accommodate everyone. At last I knew how Ángel's biddies must have felt.

Afterwards, at popular café El Gallo Azul (aka The Blue Cock), Markus introduced Madelyn and me to Beth, a fellow Australian who'd been living overseas for the past decade. Originally from Melbourne, Beth had moved to Madrid to study flamenco and, after meeting a hot Irish man, ended up getting hitched and moving to Ireland with him. She was so infatuated with flamenco, she'd set up her own school and paid for a professional teacher to fly over from London every two months. She also ran a multicultural festival and her flamenco troupe had recently been awarded a grant to go to Jerez. She'd accomplished all of the above whilst holding down a full-time job and successful marriage to an Irish hunk. I was exhausted just sitting beside her.

'Roses, Stace. That's what we need!' Madelyn declared after we left the café. She was, of course, referring to the fake kind that you stuck in your hair, although a colossal bouquet or two wouldn't have gone astray.

'I know the perfect place,' I affirmed, referring to an eclectic trinket store I'd seen near the markets where every item supposedly cost just €2 each. Every item, that was, except the shawl that Madelyn wanted that was priced at €31. Not to be outdone, I spent almost the equivalent on fake roses, dodgy eye makeup and random postcards, alongside a pretty little flamenco accessory that had always been missing in my life: the *peineta*, or ornamental hair comb.

My beautiful Spanish doll had worn a turquoise *peineta* atop her bun and if I had possessed more than 10 hairs upon my head at any one time, I would have worn one permanently as well. Just like on my doll, *peinetas* were traditionally worn underneath *mantillas*, or laced veils, most likely because they became projectile weapons whenever a dancer turned their head. In modern times, however, they were usually worn without any other accoutrements, save only for a thousand bobby pins trying to keep them in place. Whether it was something to do with *peinetas* being awfully close in spelling to *piñatas*, or the fact that they were usually made out of outrageously cheap plastic, the first time one hit the floor would inevitably be its last. That didn't stop me from buying a couple though.

'I'm telling you, Stace, they were all there!' Sebastian reiterated back at the apartment. In between mouthfuls of wine, one of my boiled potatoes, a boiled egg and some of my soccer ball-shaped Cheetos, Sebastian was recounting his adventures from the previous evening. After the smoking hot show at the Teatro featuring Andrés, Pilar and David (the magnificent male singer), most of the cast had ended up at the same bar Sebastian was at. What's more, the popular hangout was only one street away from where I was staying.

That meant I could have partied the night away surrounded by sumptuous Spanish men (with or without trouser malfunctions), but instead I had been porking out on *patatas* on my first visit to the freaking meat restaurant. I pressed Sebastian to remember details on exactly who was at the bar, but he couldn't remember the dashingly divine singer ever showing up. No doubt David had been home with his supermodel-looking wife trying to make ridiculously good-looking babies.

Bastardo.

'Are you going to Tomatito tomorrow night?' Sebastian interjected.

'Tomatito's doing a show in Jerez?!' I almost choked on a Cheeto. 'He's big time!'

It was the understatement of the century. Tomatito (no relation to beat poet Tomasito) is revered as one of the greatest flamenco guitarists of his generation. His initial break came courtesy of legendary singer Camarón (aka The Shrimp), who once needed an urgent last-minute guitarist for a gig. Although only a teenager at the time, Tomatito impressed Camarón so much, the pair ended up collaborating together for the next 18 years. Their popularity was catapulted further into the stratosphere when Tomatito's idol, Paco de Lucía, joined in the fray but sadly, since the deaths of both Camarón and Paco, Tomatito has become the last man sitting.

I'd always loved Tomatito's stage name. He might have been born José Fernández Torres, but when your father was called El Tomate (The Tomato), and your grandfather was known as El Tomate Viejo (The Old Tomato), José had no choice but to be nicknamed El Tomatito, or The Little Tomato. I dearly hoped his own son would be christened The Cherry Tomato but alas, his progeny was known only as Tomatito Hijo, or Tomatito's Son.

With no performance in the Teatro the following evening, every Tomás, Diego and Javier would be going to see Tomatito. Everyone, that was, except Madelyn and me who had plotted our final escape to Cádiz.

'How about you, Seb? Are you going?' I asked.

'Nah, I've seen him in concert before but even if I wanted to this time, I couldn't. It's completely sold out.'

That decided that then.

The one show Sebastian would not be missing out on, however, was the Teatro spectacular starring his DVD idol Rafael Campallo. A dazzling female dancer and a tall, lanky, long-haired, mustachioed rock star of a man were joining the young Joe Pesci onstage for the premiere of *Flamenco se Escribe con Jota*, or "Flamenco is Written with Jota".

'What on earth is a *jota*?' I asked Barbara before the show.

'Brace yourself.' She winked.

In hindsight, I was glad I hadn't known.

A *jota* (pronounced hot-ah) sure sounded exotic and enticing, like some kind of spicy aperitif or Spanish gigolo but, unfortunately, it was neither. The *jota* was, in fact, a folkloric partnered dance from northern Spain. Much like the secret language of the fan, this regional jig from the 18th century began as a socially acceptable way to get closer to the opposite sex and was still going strong today (hopefully for a multitude of other reasons though). The *jota* was the main inspiration for flamenco's *alegría* – or happy dance – and composer Georges Bizet ended up liking the *jota* so much, he incorporated it into the fourth act of *Carmen*. Originally, the *jota* was accompanied by the lute or Galician-style bagpipes but, luckily, neither were available for the show.

As the lights of the Teatro dimmed and the musicians assembled on stage, I watched in innocent anticipation as the three lead dancers took their places in the spotlight.

Rata tata rata tata tat.
Um … excuse me?
Rata tata tata tata rat.
What the?!
Rata tata tata tata rata tatty tatty ratty tat.
¡¡#@$%!!

Unbeknownst to me, Rock Star Man had been concealing castanets behind his back and, with very little encouragement from the crowd (i.e. me), he was off and clacking up a storm.

Fortunately, there was more to the *jota* than castanets. *La jota aragonesa*, the northern style Rock Star Man was most famous for, featured some pretty nifty moves including fancy waltz-like footwork performed at breakneck speeds and sky-high sailor kicks – all of which had to be executed without skipping a single *rata* or a *tat*. After the first number, it became increasingly clear Rock Star Man's bendy, pliable legs were the perfect candidates for the job.

Rata tata tata – bounce!

Rata tata rata – leap!

In my wildest dreams, I could not have imagined what level of training would have been required for a dancer to be so technically and rhythmically precise. The most mind-boggling part was *jota* dancers didn't play castanets like most flamenco dancers did – they played them with the castanet hanging from the middle finger instead of the thumb; a technique that required violently shaking the instrument back and forth like you were having a fit.

It was no wonder *jota* dancers shunned the loud, nail-tipped flamenco shoes of their southern contemporaries as you would never have heard any of their footwork. Instead, *jota* dancers leapt about in *alpagartas* – which sounded like garter-wearing alpacas, but they were more like a pair of *espadrilles* with ballet straps attached.

That was where Rock Star Man and tradition parted ways. He had not only modernised the *jota* by turning it into a solo dance, but he'd also grunged it up for a more contemporary audience. Instead of poufy costumes, his outfits incorporated tight-fitting black pants, suit jackets and see-through mesh tops and, rather than bounding about in clunky rope shoes, he rocked out in bright red, jazz ballet-type slippers.

Once the initial shock of the *jota* wore off, it wasn't the jaunty jumping or continuous clackers that became so disconcerting, it was the fact that the handsome Rock Star Man looked exactly like Dave Grohl from the band Foo Fighters. Not remotely, exactly. In fact, Rock Star Man looked more like Dave Grohl than Dave Grohl himself. Watching a Foo Fighter look-alike play castanets, whilst performing heel-and-toe shuffles and high sailor kicks really messed with my head after a while but he was so gloriously magnanimous, I couldn't take my eyes off him.

'Ladies!' Markus made a beeline for Madelyn and me in the foyer after the show, his eyes blazing with excitement (and it wasn't from the castanets). 'I have some great news! A friend of mine has two spare tickets for Tomatito tomorrow night!'

'Seriously?!'

'Yes! Would you like them? They cost twenty-one euros each but he's happy to part with them for fifteen.'

The moment of truth: would Madelyn and I spend our very last afternoon off exploring the sunlit, whitewashed, aquatic oasis of Cádiz, or seize our one and only opportunity of seeing The Little Tomato perform live?

'His concert in a *bodega*.' Markus continued with a playful smile. 'There'll be free sherry.' I didn't even need to look at Madelyn to know her answer.

As much as I tried, I couldn't get David Palomar – the cute *cantaor* from Andrés and Pilar's show – out of my head. What was it about the singing sensation that was so enticing, apart from his gorgeous, exotic looks, strong prominent Spanish nose (I was a sucker for those) and achingly velvet voice? One hint: his boofy hair.

Growing up in a family where flat, thin hair was the norm, it was no wonder that my mother had always had a penchant for anyone with curls. Male or female, if you sported a mop of twirly locks, you were more than okay in her books. Since I had a rapidly depleting collection of hair follicles of my own to contend with (nothing to do with being a perpetually stressed out hothead most of my life), I could appreciate the appeal. Both my mother and I wanted what we couldn't have: a thick, lustrous mane of enviable locks so bouffant, you could barely get through a doorway.

After conducting a brief mental survey of all the men I had dated (which didn't take too long), I concluded that 95 per cent of them had – or had had the potential for – boofy hair. Even those who shaved their heads never escaped my radar, as I had innately known when they possessed the magical gene and would spend our entire relationship encouraging them to become boofheads. Personality-wise, at least, my wishes had always come true.

As I meandered back to Spanish Melrose Place, I heard the familiar strains of "Love Is in the Air" blasting from a passing car. It was the theme song from the movie *Strictly Ballroom* – one of the boofy-haired stars of which (Antonio Vargas) taught the very first flamenco workshop I attended. I took it as a confirmed sign that *el amor estará en el aire* – love was most certainly soon to be in the air.

¡Arsa!

28

CONTRA EL SONIQUETE
Against the Groove

'We have to take our shoes off.'

'What?!' Madelyn and I whispered to the Dutch student, having only just finished strapping ours on.

'Blanca's just asked us to remove them. She's going to show us a warm-up in bare feet.'

I was glad I'd left my stinkier pair back at the apartment for the day.

'Ladies, let us begin.' Blanca gathered the students around and, for the next 10 minutes, we circled and pointed our footsies whilst Blanca enlightened us about how Maasai tribes had always known the importance of looking after their feet for balance and posture. The Maasai even undertook regular exercises to keep their feet in shape, much like we were doing, Blanca explained. (I couldn't imagine the Maasai would be too keen on how flamenco dancers regularly tortured their own soles, though.)

Aside from the teachings of Ángel, Blanca and the entire Maasai community, warm-ups and cool-downs weren't always on offer at dance workshops. To save precious teaching time, instructors often left it up to students as to whether they stretched beforehand, afterwards or not at all. The preference seemed to be to throw participants straight into a sequence of blazing footwork and *muy rápido* arm movements that rendered students so shaky, they could barely lift any limbs for several hours afterwards.

'The steps are nothing by themselves,' Blanca assured us after announcing she would not be revising any of the previous day's choreography. 'It is the *feel* that is most important. This is what you need to learn.' I was certainly feeling something alright.

'*Aiiiiiiiiiiiiiiiiiiiiiiiiiiiiiiiiiiiiiiiiiiiiii!!!*'

Once again, to match the guitarist's excessively loud speakers, the singer's microphone had been cranked up to deafen. Shrill flamenco cries brought tears to my eyes and not in a good way. Before my eardrums completely shattered, I marched over to tell the singer to turn the freaking sound down, but she stood up and exited the room before I could get to her. So, when no one was looking, I turned the volume down myself.

I had literally been away from my spot for 30 seconds but it was enough for the crankiest, tallest German in class to sweep in and claim it as her own. All week, I'd been trying to avoid her as she spat and hissed at the other students to keep 10 abreast per row and to stay in their position, but clearly Frau Cow had no intentions of heeding her own advice. With no other option, I took her old spot up the back but when I couldn't see Blanca, I was finally forced to improvise. When I briefly stepped away for a sip of water towards the end of the lesson, Frau Cow reclaimed her original spot, forcing me back to mine. I was starting to miss the biddies.

Since Ángel's workshop, Madelyn had been pestering me to teach her some of the steps from the *martinete*. As it was the only set choreography she was going to learn for the week, I happily agreed and we spent the afternoon grooving up a storm in the old stone courtyard. There was no need for *palmas* – we simply danced our hearts out to the rhythmic hammering and drilling from the construction site next door, like the early flamenco pioneers would have done. Ángel would have been *increíblemente* proud of us.

'All set, Stace?' Madelyn knocked on my front door. 'Markus is ready and Sim's just arrived.'

'Sorry, coming now!' I grabbed my scarf and scurried out to join the others for the lengthy uphill trek to the *bodega* where Tomatito was performing. By the time we arrived, we were one of the very last to join the snaking queue of students huddled together in the cold night air.

Once nestled inside the entrance to the charming Bodega de los Apóstoles, however, we were instantly enveloped by a warm, welcome glow from cosily lit lanterns dangling from the wooden rafters above. With no allocated seating for the show, our plan of attack was to grab a table well away from one of the large brick pillars in order to enjoy an uninterrupted view of the stage. Coincidentally, that was everybody else's plan as well and once every audience member had their complimentary glass of paint-stripping *fino* in hand, they broke into a mad dash to secure the best seats in the house.

'How about this one, guys?' Markus yelled out from across the cellar, having thrown himself at one of the tables to the side of the stage.

'Perfect!' we responded, until we saw an even better option near the front.

'I'll get it!' I sprang into action, hurling my jacket over one of the chairs.

Plonk. An expensive-looking handbag slammed down onto the tablecloth. I immediately looked up to see who had challenged my territory and found myself face-to-face with the defiant Frau Cow.

'Sorry,' I declared with as much mock sarcasm as I could muster, 'looks like I beat you to it.'

The entitled bovine was having none of it. 'No! This is *our* table,' she hissed.

'But I was here first!' I protested and signalled to the rest of the group to join me, but they were too gripped with fear and *indecisión*. Just then, Frau Cow's browbeaten husband arrived, puffing with exertion. The smug look on her face said it all. I scowled as offensively as I could and stormed back to join the others.

Thank goodness for Markus. Whilst I had been fighting for our rights to recline, he'd managed to secure us lots more free sherry. Before I could relish watching The Little Tomato perform though, a quick detour to the restroom was in order. I just had to find it first. In a promising-looking hallway up the back of the *bodega*, I found what I assumed to be the entrance to the powder room but, when I barged in, I found myself face-to-face with one of Tomatito's younger guitarists. The handsome *tocaor* was so nonchalant at having an anaemic-looking, Andy Warhol-doppelgänger invade his dressing room, he simply looked up, smiled and continued to play his guitar. God bless Spanish men.

As I returned to the table, the lights began to dim and the capacity crowd went wild as one by one Tomatito's all-male band – in matching black, long-sleeved shirts and trousers – filed onto the stage, followed by the star attraction himself. Then, with a flick of his long, curly black hair and a disarming grin, Tomatito began to play. The spell he wove over the audience, combined with his incredible dexterity and sublime musicality, never let up the entire evening.

Tomatito didn't generally accompany anyone other than vocalists and guitarists, so it was a lovely surprise when a local dancer was invited onstage for the final *bulería* of the evening. Rumour had it the young beanpole of a man had been refused entry to our favourite pub the previous night for urinating on the bar but, quite frankly, that only added to his appeal. With his lengthy raven hair flying all over the place, the *bailaor* ferociously threw his testosterone-fuelled boots into every *compás*, resulting in a thunderous standing ovation. Even Frau Cow looked impressed.

After the show, to commemorate the evening Markus, Simone, Madelyn and I posed for a photograph in front of a giant Tío Pepe wine bottle jauntily dressed as a flamenco guitarist. For the less inebriated out there, Tío Pepe is one of Spain's most successful sherry producers – an impressive feat considering most of its products are the bone dry, straw-coloured, parched earth-tasting *finos*.

Owning a wildly successful sherry empire was clearly not enough for the Tío Pepe dynasty. Pepe's nephew, Manuel María González Ángel, was not only a man of many monikers but was apparently the first Spaniard to install electricity and running water in the nation's industrial warehouses. Not to be outdone by either initiative or name, one of Manuel's sons, Pedro Nolasco González de Soto, was allegedly responsible for introducing the sports of polo, tennis and clay pigeon shooting to Spain, all whilst finding the time to father 13 children.

One of those children, Manuel María González Gordon – also known as the Marqués de Bonanza – wrote the book *Sherry: The Noble Wine*, which became revered as "The Bible of Sherry". If that wasn't impressive enough, one of *his* sons, Mauricio González-Gordon y Díez, was an avid environmentalist who somehow persuaded General Franco not to turn a huge tract of wilderness on their family property into a eucalyptus farm destined for the paper mill. That land is now known as the UNESCO World Heritage-listed Doñana National Park: one of Europe's largest nature reserves, under which the fabled city of Atlantis is rumoured to be buried. (On reflection, however, without the incredible women of the Tío Pepe family tree who devoted their lives to being endlessly pregnant and nurturing such brilliant offspring, I'm not sure all of the above achievements may have come to pass.)

With an entire town of culinary choices at our disposal, there was only one venue everyone wanted to convene at to meet Sebastian after the show – the fricking meat restaurant, of course. Sure, I may have washed down a plate of pork sirloin smothered in Roquefort cheese resting on a bed of crispy *patatas* with a glass of sweet *dulce* sherry, but that hadn't meant I enjoyed it.

Just as Markus, Sebastian and I were leaving the premises, we were stopped by a group of young British and South African students. The boys were training to be pilots at a nearby flying school and if they weren't so gosh-darned underage, I might have offered to be their flight attendant. There was no time to join them for a drink, however, as it was almost midnight, which meant only one thing: the *peñas* were about to open.

In the various murky online videos I'd seen (when I wasn't watching practical jokes), *peñas* were usually depicted as crowded, smoke-filled basement dives but the reality of Jerez's Peña la Bulería could not have been more refreshing. Its exterior whitewashed, wrought iron façade instantly reminded me of Manuel's academy entrance and inside, there wasn't a waft of smoke to be found throughout its neat, elegant performance space.

Adhering to tradition, the stage was about the size of a handkerchief and I watched in slack-jawed wonder as three singers, a guitarist, two young *palmeros*, a young girl, a random old man and a middle-aged lady crammed onto the raised platform. It wasn't until I noticed that most of the performers wore the slipper-type shoes that the bouncy Dave Grohl man wore that I became a little edgy.

Sensing my disorientation, Markus leant over and whispered in my ear. 'There probably won't be any dancers tonight, Stace. *Peñas* are more about showcasing local guitarists and singers.' No dancers most likely meant there'd be no castanets. I visibly relaxed into my seat, knowing I might well have been about to witness history in the making. *Peñas* were the type of venues where artists like Camarón de la Isla and Paco de Lucía began their careers; a place where serious musicians went to hone their craft in the art of *puro* flamenco – and in comfortable shoes, no less.

'That was great!' I enthused after the show. 'Does anyone want another drink before we go?'

'Stace, there's another set to go,' Sebastian explained. 'We're only halfway through!'

It was 2 a.m. If I'd stayed out a moment longer, I would have turned into a vague space cadet of a pumpkin (well, more than usual). Leaving the *entusiastas dedicados* behind, I sauntered back to the apartment to the harmonious sounds of a rubbish collection in full swing throughout the moonlit streets of Jerez.

29

OTRA VEZ
Again

I could put it off no longer. My family back home deserved to know that not only was I still alive and intermittently well, but I had yet to run off with any charismatic Casanovas. I knew they would be bitterly disappointed with the latter, or would have been had any of the public pay phones in town been working. I could have sent a text message to them from my international SIM card, but there were only so many shenanigans you could squeeze into 120 characters. When an internet café offered to charge me €2 just to sit in their phone booth, let alone pick up the receiver and dial another country, I was forced to do what any self-respecting backpacker would do – I jumped online and sent a mass impersonal email peppered with intriguing Spanish keyboard-induced punctuation to loved ones instead.

With a few minutes of internet time still up my sleeve, I decided it couldn't hurt to do a bit of undercover *investigación* on the gorgeous Teatro singer from Andrés Peña's show whilst

I was there. I was woefully underprepared for what I was about to discover.

David Palomar, whose first name was actually Jesús, first began learning flamenco guitar in his hometown of Cádiz, but never had the patience to pursue it any further so he took up dancing, but later admitted it was more to flirt with the *chicas* than the floorboards. It was only when David heard the incredible Camarón sing live that he knew he'd found his true calling. Several years later, life came full circle when David was awarded the prestigious Camarón de la Isla Award for his own vocal prowess.

The list of flamenco stars he had already shared the stage with was extraordinary. David had sung for the hip-hop-loving Isabel Bayón, and Farruquito (whose workshop I was missing), toured with Paco Peña and even performed at the Cádiz Carnaval – I assumed – in a fabulous costume. However, for such a veteran performer, it didn't get any easier and, as each year passed, David confessed to becoming increasingly wracked with stage fright. I was sure I could have found a way to have helped him with that.

Further internet "research" revealed no evidence of a wedding ring in any of David's online photos. I prayed he would do one more festival show so I could "casually" bump into him in a bar afterwards wearing nothing but my knickers. He was, after all, only a year younger than me (cougar alert!).

I stopped to reread the part about David's tour with Paco Peña. Instantly, my mind raced back to the Paco show in Brisbane where I first laid eyes on Ángel – or more specifically – his thighs. After the performance, Paco's troupe was invited up to the theatre's main foyer to sign autographs. It took an enormous vat of wine for me to muster up the courage to join the extensive queue of fans, let alone speak to the man of my dreams. Finally, when it was my turn, I thrust my programme into Ángel's face and nervously blurted out that I, too, was a flamenco dancer. I hoped his lack of response was because he didn't hear or understand me but, either way, I realised it was best to just shut my clackers and move on. A young male singer was the last to sign my programme. It was only when we made eye contact that I noticed how exotically handsome he was. As he returned my programme, he gave me a mischievous wink.

When I was about to leave, I noticed the singer on his own at the bar. With no Ángels around to distract me, I snuck over and told him how much I'd enjoyed his singing. (Okay, I may not have *watched* him sing, but I certainly had heard him.) The most handsomest of men then ran a hand through his dark, wavy hair and broke into a huge Spanish smile; his flirty eyes a-twinkling all over the place. There were so many sparks flying between us, it was all I could do not to spontaneously combust.

As last drinks were called, I could feel the singer's infectious energy drawing me towards him, imploring me to surrender to the moment and the *pasión intensa* between us. So what did I do? I freaked out, kissed him goodbye and fled silently into the night, wondering what might have been. I really did have to work on that.

Back at the internet café in Jerez, a frenzied image search of the singers from my first Paco Peña show confirmed my most ardent of suspicions: the gorgeous man who had flirted with me at the bar back in Brisbane had, in fact, been David Palomar himself!! *Arrgghhh!!* With no time to waste, I looked up his details and immediately sent him a badly translated message, gushing and fan-girling about his recent show at the Teatro and how I'd had the pleasure of meeting him in Brisbane once. I also enquired as to whether he had any further performances coming up in Jerez. I figured I would either get a reply or a restraining order.

'It is the singer's job to express his or her self freely and our job to translate their words through our bodies in abstract ways.' Even Blanca had vocalists on the brain. 'I grew up in a traditional flamenco school where you were taught not to count, but to feel. You must always listen to your singer and be ready to improvise. What and how you dance should always be in direct response to the vocals.'

It was a completely foreign concept to me. With little or no *cantaors* accompanying lessons back in Australia, most students learnt set choreographies to either recorded music or an up-and-coming guitarist, leaving little room for improvisation. No wonder Sebastian had always urged me to listen to flamenco every waking moment. It was the only way to truly absorb the *compás*.

'I don't like anyone who dances over the top of the singer,' Blanca explained. (She obviously didn't mind it when a guitarist chewed their lunch over the top of her teaching, though.) 'This is not the traditional way. I could teach you some steps without singing, but dancing just to rhythm is not true flamenco.'

Madelyn suddenly excused herself, feigning illness.

'Are you okay, Mads?' I mumbled from the sidelines.

'My nose is running a bit, Stace, but to be honest I've just got to get out of here.' She sighed and took off down the stairs. I, however, was determined to last the distance and, whilst a handful of fellow students managed to fashion a few impressive steps to the singer's *letras*, my *mantón* and I became nothing but a big, hot tangled mess. At least we were on the same page.

The perplexity continued as I ricocheted around the aisles of the Supermercado afterwards, wondering why on earth I was there. Finally, as I went to measure my produce like the locals did, the weighing machine decided to pack it in. Being unable to decipher the digital instructions, I was forced to kiss my basket of deliciously fresh vegetables goodbye and say, '*Hola!*' to yet another packet of frozen peas (where had they all gone?!), consoling myself with the fact that at least they wouldn't be sharing my freezer with the Easter Bunny. As I paid for the peas, the unofficial Spanish anthem of "I Will Survive" began pumping through the store's speakers. Just like David Hasselhoff's "alleged" popularity in Germany, I sure hoped Gloria Gaynor knew just how much she was admired in Spain.

In her premiere show at the Teatro that evening, the utterly captivating Mercedes Ruiz promised to share everything from her heart with her audience in *Mi Último Secreto* and, boy, did she deliver. Throughout her five jaw-dropping solos, the classically stunning dancer alternated between elegant precision and frenzied passion. So, too, her eye-catching costumes spanned a kaleidoscope of colours and textures: vivid reds, pastel lavender satins and lace, a crisp white pant suit, and a showstopping blue-and-purple *bata de cola* garnished with a turquoise fan.

After an abundantly satisfying show, Mercedes had one more secret to reveal. In the midst of a unanimous standing ovation, she gestured for the crowd to quieten and proceeded to profusely thank each and every one of us for our collective attention, enthusiasm and support. Up until then, I'd never seen nor heard anyone so genuinely grateful for their audience's embrace. If you hadn't already adored Mercedes beforehand, you had no chance after that.

Months after I returned to Australia, I was flicking through photographs from the Trafalgar tour of Spain when I happened across an image from the one and only flamenco show in our itinerary – and was stunned by just how familiar the principal dancers looked. Closer inspection revealed that just 10 years prior, in a tourist-ridden *tablao* deep in the heart of Barcelona, I had witnessed the blossoming careers of both Mercedes Ruiz and Andrés Peña – who were also allegedly an item at the time. If that wasn't freaking full circle, nothing was.

30

EL DESTINO
If It's Meant to Be

'Oh hi, Gabriela!' I ran into our landlord on the way out the front gate, after having been awoken early by the most brutal construction noise of the week.

'*Qué tal*, Eh-Stacey.' We double-kissed hello.

'Hey, Gabriela, I've got to ask, how do you handle this relentless racket every day?'

'Zis noise? We have no choice, Eh-Stacey. When we moved here, there waz no construction anywhere. Now it eez next door and zere eez no escape!'

'Do you know when they'll finish?' I implored.

Gabriela shook her head. 'Believe me, zey are in no hurry to be done. Last year, zey worked one month on, one month off ze whole year.'

'That must have driven you crazy! Is there anything you can do about it?'

'No. We just have to put up weez it.' Gabriela looked

around before continuing. 'One time one of ze men accidentally knocked down one of our walls.'

'They what?!'

'Jes. It took zem a year to feex it. Ze wall broke our stairs, which are still broken today and it damaged ze antenna.' That explained why Madelyn and Evie had more television channels than me. Gabriela patted my hand. 'Don't worry, Eh-Stacey. Zis eez nothing. Small thingz like zis alwayz happen. We will survive.'

Someone really should write a song about that.

With our chronically intensifying colds and confusion, Madelyn and I struggled to get motivated for Blanca's workshop and, in the end, Madelyn decided she'd get more out of photographing birds than floundering about perturbed, leaving me to fly the Aussie flag *sola*.

'Girls, gather around and listen to me please,' Blanca requested after seeing how distressed some of us had become trying to avoid being strangled by our shawls.

'Your *mantón* is a mirror. If you're angry, your *mantón* will get angry and not work with you. You have to hold love in your heart at all times.'

The students and I looked at each other sheepishly.

'It's the same attitude you need in life. If someone gives you a poisonous smile, smile back with your heart. Say "no thanks" to anger. Have good feelings towards everyone and they'll treat you as your *mantón* will.'

It finally dawned on me why I had chosen Blanca's workshop. It wasn't to learn how to improvise or free myself from a wayward piece of polyester; it was to spend a week in the divine presence of a most benevolent matriarch as she bestowed her majestic wisdom – aka the *Tao of Mantón* – upon us all. It was obvious Blanca cared enormously for her students, and for flamenco, but what good was any of it if you weren't also a nice person? (Frau Cow: take note.) With her generous display of poise, grace and humility, Blanca had covertly been teaching us how to become ladies long after we'd hung up our flamenco shoes and that, in all sincerity, was worth much more than any steps would ever be.

'Girls, do you want to meet me at the Senovilla store this afternoon?' came the text from Simone.

'Do we what!!' I instantly replied on behalf of Madelyn and myself.

Finding flamenco shoes that perfectly fitted was akin to the quest for the Holy Grail – or in our case – the Holy Nail. Having an entire shoe store filled with a plethora of gorgeous handmade creations was the stuff dreams were made of, so long as we were ready to make some crucial decisions.

- Type of material – *Leather or suede*
- Type of fastenings – *T-shaped, X-shaped, single or double straps*
- Style of heel – *Standard, carrete (curved) or cubano (short and thick)*
- Height of heel – *The minimum 5cm; the maximum a lofty 7cm*
- Material of heel – *Exposed wood or material that matched the rest of the shoe*
- Patterns and embellishments – *Roses, stripes, polka dots or embroidered flames up the sides that made it look like your feet were on fire*
- Colour – *The hardest choice of all!*

Ultimately, only when a dancer had a perfectly colour-coordinated pair of flamenco shoes for every single costume and practice skirt she owned could she ever say she had enough.

When I first began lessons in Brisbane, the only way to order shoes was from either overseas or online; the latter of which was fraught with peril. Once, after I ordered a semi-professional black suede pair from a leading Spanish website, I was slogged an additional $120 just to get the shoes through Australian Customs because some #@$% on the other end forgot to mark them as a "gift". You could imagine my delight when the shoes arrived and didn't fit. I offered to send them back to the company to see how they'd like the extra charge, but they begged me not to and instantly refunded the cost of the shoes (excluding the customs fee), suggesting I donate them to a local dance school instead. What I didn't know at the time was that suede took much longer to break in than leather and within a few short weeks of wearing them around the house, the shoes moulded perfectly to my feet. It was just a pity I forgot to tell the manufacturers.

Back in Jerez, as Simone, Madelyn and I stepped into the Senovilla showroom, we became instantly enamoured with an orgy of sparkly flamenco shoes in every conceivable colour and design. What's more, the founding owner, Miguel Senovilla, just so happened to be visiting for the day and proceeded to fuss over the three of us like royalty, even going so far as to personally measure our feet. 'You mean it's not normal for your toes to go numb after an hour of footwork?!' Madelyn and I exclaimed, stunned to discover we'd been wearing the wrong-sized shoes most of our dancing lives.

The special attention lavished upon us – alongside the lush, heady scent of jasmine wafting through the store windows – made for an exhilarating mix and caused me to go characteristically and spectacularly overboard. Before I could help myself, I had ordered three pairs of *profesional* standard, *cubano*-heeled shoes priced at €171 each ($230 AUD at the time). Each work of art was to be meticulously handmade and shipped to Australia as I paid for them and, after just eight months, I became the proud owner of a pair of black *negro* shoes with a 5-centimetre heel and cross-over straps, shiny *rojo sangre* (blood-red) shoes with parallel straps and an exposed wooden heel, and pure white *blanco* shoes with parallel straps and a matching white heel. Pure bliss in every box.

In the hopes that Madelyn would give in to my endless pleading and let me borrow her laptop before we headed off to the Teatro, I got ready super early and skulked around outside her apartment. *¡Misión cumplida!* When I was safely back in my lounge room, with sweaty palms and no one looking over my shoulder, I logged into Myspace and almost sent my bowl of steamed vegetables flying when there, in my inbox, was a reply from David Palomar. I stared vacantly and unblinkingly at the walls until the shock wore off. When that didn't work, I took a swig of Evie's brandy and clicked to open his Spanish reply.

Was it a good response? I had no idea, considering I didn't speak the language, but at least it was from David or at least I hoped it was. With all the exclamation marks contained within the message, it could well have been a cease and desist from his wife/girlfriend/grandmother. Multiple websites conspired to come up with vaguely garbled translations, from which I deciphered the following: for the flamenco festival, David had had only two appearances and sadly, his most recent performance with Andrés Peña had been his last – although he did have another show coming up in his hometown at the end of the month. The most exciting part was, though, it had most *definitely* been David that I'd met at the bar in Australia all those years ago (not that he'd remembered, of course). He signed off the message with, '*Kisses and look after yourself!!!*'

Kisses.

All I could focus on were his kisses.

Sure, I could have interpreted them as the friendly Spanish salutation they typically were, but I always preferred to take most offers of lip smacking from the opposite sex quite literally.

'Ready, Stace?' Madelyn called out. 'I'll chuck my laptop back in the apartment before we go.'

'Give me a couple of minutes!' I hollered out a little too hastily. Just like the plumbing, the archaic internet was in no mood to be rushed. When at last I was reconnected, I looked up the date of David's first show, held on the fifth night of the festival. When I could have been salivating over Señor Palomar at a late-night venue, I had shunned the meat restaurant to retire early in a futile attempt to catch up on sleep. Since I would be long gone before David's upcoming show in Cádiz, all I could do was luxuriate in his virtual kisses. Were you even allowed to proffer them if you were married?!

Then it struck me. I'd only checked to see if David had been wearing a wedding ring on his *left* hand, like Australians did, oblivious to the fact that in Europe many cultures wore symbols of betrothal on their *right*. Further trusty "research" of David's images revealed he almost always wore a ring on his right hand – just like Ángel, who was most definitely off the market.

Fantástico.

The fiery, terry towelling-clad dancer I had witnessed in Seville was presenting the second final show of the festival: *un tributo dramático* to the women of Federico García Lorca's poems. I assumed her musician husband would have been in her band but, as the curtains lifted, he was nowhere to be seen. Actually he was – he was sitting in the audience beaming with pride – but that was beside the point.

Up until then, I'd been shamefully ignorant about the legend that was Lorca. Thanks to Wikipedia, I knew he was outrageously and tragically killed at the age of 38 at the beginning of the Spanish Civil War sadly, like many others, due to either his political views or homosexuality, or both. I also knew his poems and plays were fervently embraced the world over, but that was about the extent of my knowledge.

As the curtains opened, I couldn't help but notice an enormous number of women's flamenco shoes piled high atop a grand piano. During one of the solos, shoes then fell from the ceiling and, at another point, shoes were thrown onto the stage from the wings. Forget saving for months to afford a single pair, I could have just helped myself to multiple options during the curtain call. According to the programme, a well-known shoe manufacturer from Madrid had supplied all of the footwear. I sure hoped they weren't being returned afterwards.

When the production finished, a Spanish student sitting beside me had tears rolling down her face. '*Qué bonita,*' she whispered in hushed adoration. The female dancer's unique, intense and potent style of flamenco was certainly the consummate vehicle to convey the struggle, pain and rebellion of Lorca's women. I just wish I'd known what they were. It wasn't until much later that I found out one of Lorca's most famous poems was about a shoemaker's wife. Ah.

31

DESAHOGO
Sweet Relief

'Right!' I decided. 'That's it!' No amount of testosterone-fuelled construction noise, nor the fact that it was Friday the 13th (yet again) was going to dampen my spirits. Blanca had seemingly taught all the choreography she was going to for the week and, with our graduation ceremony still another day away, I would be damned if Madelyn and I were going to miss out on our very last opportunity to bump into David Palomar in his hometown. I bounded out of bed and tapped on Madelyn's window.

'Mmmm??' came the sleepy reply.

'Get up, Mads! We're going to Cádiz!'

She was instantly awake. 'Give me five minutes!'

With only moments to make the lunchtime train, Madelyn and I power-walked past the headless male torso roundabout and down to the station, only to discover that the advertised 12:08 p.m. train did not, in fact, exist. Instead, we were compelled to wait for the following one scheduled for 12:35 p.m. At least there *was* another one.

By some stroke of luck, by the entrance to the terminal, I found the only working payphone in the whole of Spain and called home for a quick chat. Literally one minute into the conversation, an announcement came over the PA system: the next train to Cádiz was about to leave. I shouted a harried goodbye to my family member, slammed down the receiver and hurled Madelyn and myself onto the nearest carriage. Fortunately, there would be no sitting on the floor pretending to be poor, sad *gitanas* as there were plenty of seats available.

It was no wonder. Ten minutes later, the train still hadn't moved. I longingly eyed off the restrooms on the platform, but knew if I had taken a single step towards any of them, the train would have immediately departed. When I eventually found the on-board facilities, I panicked not knowing whether I was allowed to use them before departure or not, or whether that only applied to boats and planes.

'At last!' Madelyn and I exclaimed when the train pulled out of Jerez and I wasn't fined for any *indiscreciones públicas*. Miles of rural farmland and desolate fields kept us entertained for the next hour, alongside a couple of bogan, beer-swilling Aussie louts who were desperately trying to get their international SIM cards to work. As Madelyn kindly offered to assist them, I pretended I was a mute foreign exchange student from the Czech Republic.

Our landlady Gabriela had warned us that the coastal mecca of Cádiz would either be very windy or warm when we arrived. As Madelyn and I exited the train station, a blustering hot breeze smacked us right in the face.

¡Bienvenido a Cádiz!

'Let's grab some maps first,' Madelyn suggested, gesturing to a nearby tourist office. Even though it was only a short walk from the station into Cádiz's Old Town, with my track record we may well have ended up in Portugal. With fresh maps in hand, Madelyn and I made a beeline straight to one of the grandest attractions in the region: the Catedral de Cádiz – also known as the Santa y Apostólica Iglesia Catedral de la Santa Cruz de Cádiz – aka the Catedral Nueva, for those adverse to a little verbosity.

Flanked by palm trees, the majestic church boasted towering turrets, a yellow-domed cupola roof and a split colour sequence that looked like the building had been dipped in chocolate. I would have happily basked in the cathedral's rich historical significance – or at least in the affectionate sunlight outside – if there wasn't an embarrassment of touristy trinket stores nearby.

After moving house as a child, my beautiful Spanish doll had become irretrievably and heartbreakingly lost and I'd been on a mission to find a suitable replacement ever since; a wonderfully sentimental notion that had no chance of being realised when the only figurines for sale in Cádiz looked like they were from Carnaval.

'*¡Olé, guapa!*' a voice cried out from across the plaza. I didn't even bother to turn around to see who had dispatched the playful compliment, convinced that the Spanish equivalent of 'Hey good-looking!' was intended for Madelyn and not the squat, short-haired, Mumsy-looking lady beside her (unless they were into that sort of thing in Cádiz).

'Oh my God.' Madelyn exhaled when we finally caught our first glimpse of the Atlantic Ocean. 'It's stunning!'

'Mads,' I responded, inhaling the sparkling sea air, 'this is the first time I actually feel like I'm on holiday.'

'We should have come sooner,' Madelyn concurred as her huge photographic lens began whirring and clicking away. Perched high upon an old stone wall in the enchanting warmth of the sun, we gazed dreamily into the aquatic abyss as seagulls soared above and water lapped gently at the pebbles below. If Cádiz wasn't paradise, it was darn tootin' close.

'Let's head up there next,' Madelyn suggested, pointing to a nearby hill.

Whitewashed edifices lined the quietly meandering avenues as their chalky exteriors shimmered brilliantly in the sunlight. For some reason, the steep streets were all but deserted except for Madelyn and me and an enormous truck attempting a U-turn. Such was the width of the laneway he was contending with, the driver's ambitious plans for a single turn quickly escalated into a 100-point turn. Madelyn and I stood transfixed as the determined driver repeatedly drove back and forth, with the truck's engine a-revving and breaks a-squealing, only to move a few *centímetros* at a time.

'Imagine doing that every day,' Madelyn mused when at last the truck driver succeeded in his mission.

'I'd rather eat gluten,' I declared.

'Look, Stace! It's the flamenco tiles we saw in Arcos!' Madelyn raced over to a nearby shop window. 'I'll have to get some!'

CERRADO – the sign on the door smugly proclaimed.

'Bloody *siestas*!' Madelyn waved her fist. We agreed to return later in the afternoon, if ever we found the place again. We continued onto the summit where, naturally, my blood sugar decided to plummet so, to avoid me becoming a Cranky Franky, Madelyn suggested we pop back down the hill and grab lunch at one of the cafés by the cathedral. Wisely, we chose the largest, most commercial-looking restaurant on the strip in the hopes they would cater for a gastronomically challenged *guapa*.

'*Qué quieren pedir?*' the waiter asked.

'Ah yes. Um ... *quiero jamón con huevos y* something *y tortilla con* ... um whatever that word is.' I pointed at the menu, marvelling at my increasing grasp of the local lingo. 'Oh and *no puedo comer trigo!*' I added. The waiter looked confused.

'*No PUE-do COM-er TRI-go?*' I ventured again.

The waiter shook his head, said something to the effect of '*Lalalalalala de lalalalalala*', then gestured something equally indecipherable.

With my "hangry" pants well and truly on, I pleaded for mercy. '*Por favor. No trigo! Gracias.*' And with that, the waiter took our menus and left.

'I wonder what bull tastes like,' Madelyn pondered, having ordered her first ever *toro* dish of the trip. I prayed it was loaded with gluten so I wouldn't have to find out.

Not long after, the verdict was in. 'Delicious!' Madelyn declared, dipping the accompanying *chocos fritos* into her savoury stew. A cold, uninspired, flat piece of *tortilla* sustained me until a plate of *jamón* arrived. I wasn't sure what part of '*No puedo comer TRIGO!*' the waiter hadn't understood. Actually I had – *nada*. What were formerly a few pieces of Porky Pig had been coated in glutenous breadcrumbs and deep-fried within an inch of their lives. Madelyn ended up enjoying them as much as her stew.

There was no point even attempting to use the restaurant's restrooms. Their one and only toilet had so much paper piled up inside the bowl, it practically had its own postcode. On the way back to the table, a big fat sign on the footpath caught my eye welcoming potential customers to the restaurant IN ENGLISH. On the flip side, was a plastic sleeve filled with English menus. As Madelyn and I had walked in via the side entrance, we'd completely missed the tourist-friendly welcome out the front. To say I was *furiosa* was an understatement.

'Did you enjoy your lunch, ladies?' our no-longer-exclusively-Spanish waiter asked us in perfect English as he collected the bill. 'The stew was great, thanks,' Madelyn blurted out, before breaking into a sprint as I stormed across the plaza.

'Mads, I've still gotta go to the toilet!' I lamented when she finally caught up with me.

'Alright, love, there's gotta be a Macca's around here someplace.' Instead, we found a Burger King with a toilet door so inescapable, it took a full five minutes to pick the lock to freedom. I assumed a crowbar was supplied with every burger purchase.

With every kind of bodily function well and truly out of the way, Madelyn and I had to get a wriggle on if we wanted to continue – or indeed truly start – exploring the Old Town.

Unfortunately, due to time constraints, a visit to Cádiz's more modern New Town would not be on the cards; neither would anyone be taking us to Funky Town. Our plan instead was to walk the circumference of the water-bound central district before we immersed ourselves in its exotic interior – all whilst we remained on high alert for any sightings of Señor Palomar.

As we set off, the tall, imposing shipping wall that enveloped the Old City afforded only rare glimpses of the turquoise nirvana beyond, allowing Madelyn and me to focus on more immediate attractions – like mosaic-tiled fountains filled with urinating cherubs that I dearly hoped would not have any influence over my highly impressionable bladder.

'What the hell is this place?!' I blurted out when we reached the entrance to Parque Genovés. Try as we might, Madelyn and I could not recall ingesting any hallucinogens earlier in the day or, in fact, ever but it was the only explanation we could come up with to justify such a trippy fantasyland by the sea. At the park's entrance was a promenade of towering topiary trees; the branches of which had been magically sculpted to resemble swirls of soft serve ice cream, rounded Paddle Pops and cubes stacked upon one another. To the right was La Gruta – a man-made waterfall, lake and cave that would one day be furnished with dinosaur statues. Down by the water was what looked to be active vegetable plots and an abandoned amphitheatre. All that was missing was Johnny Depp as The Mad Hatter and/or Edward Scissorhands.

It was hard to believe Parque Genovés hadn't always been so vividly verdant. In the early days, it was originally known as Paseo del Perejil, or Parsley Promenade, due to its sparse lack of vegetation. A few decades later, the barren grounds received a leafy makeover to become Paseo de las Delicias, or Promenade of Delights, before a green thumb by the name of Genovés y Puig transformed it into the botanical fairyland of today. Flocks of ducks, geese and parrots now happily call the park home, which is probably why a sizeable stray cat population has also moved in. As Madelyn and I strolled throughout the gardens, we spotted little bowls of food and water under the topiary trees, no doubt provided by kind locals offering alternative dining options for the park's resident Cheshires.

Seeing all the cat crunchies inevitably gave me the munchies and I steered Madelyn into La Prensa, the nearest bar, for a quick fuel stop. Their *tortilla* turned out to be one of the tastiest I'd eaten, but it wasn't a patch on their English menu translations. If a customer was baying for bread, they could order it *media tostada* (average toasted) or *tostada entera* (toasted finds out). If Madelyn had been anticipating a plate of animal innards, she wouldn't have been able to go past *paté a las finas hierbas*, or "paté to the fine ones you boil". For a dash of dairy, the *queso de cabra curado*, or "old cheese of goat" sure sounded enticing, but was not to be outdone by the noble-sounding *boquerones en vinagre*, or "vinegar big holes", which sounded nothing like the marinated anchovies they were supposed to be. It was either a classic example of the Cádizian sense of humour, or the bar owners had been using the same online translation tools as I had.

With tummies full of *tortilla*, Madelyn and I were primed and ready to hit the beach. What the nearby Playa de la Caleta, or Beach of the Cove lacked in size, it sure made up for with picture-postcard charm. Children squealed with delight as they played upon the soft beige sand whilst their parents watched from underneath shady umbrellas at a nearby café. At the end of a long enclosed walkway, an enormous Great Gatsby-esque whitewashed pavilion jutted out over the water's edge. In its heyday, the elegant, hexagonal edifice housed a luxury spa, but had since been transformed into the headquarters of the intriguing-sounding Centre for Subaquatic Archaeology.

There was only one spectacle missing from the thoroughly pleasant vista: swimmers. Not a single *persona* was in the water; not even to bathe in the shallows. *Nadie*, it seemed, would *nadar*. Mothers and children hovered about the shoreline, but none would venture even a toenail further. It wasn't the hottest day on record but the sun was sultry enough, and the wind mild enough, for beachgoers to be in their summer gear. But still, no one swam. The only rationale Madelyn and I could conjure up for all the landlubbing was that a veritable treasure trove of venomous sea creatures must have been lurking just below the surface.

The truth was spectacularly more bizarre.

Remember the scene from James Bond's *Die Another Day* where Halle Berry sashays out of the ocean in an orange bikini? I don't, because I've never seen it and never want to, but the infamous scene was supposedly filmed at Playa de la Caleta. One could only assume the water has been declared sacred and permanently out of bounds since Miss Berry frolicked about in it.

La Caleta had another unusual claim to fame, but you would need your hip flask for this one. Rumour had it that every single stone on the beach had been christened. You heard me correctly. Some group of wildly creative souls with an inordinate amount of spare time (who may or may not have worked for the Centre for Subaquatic Archaeology, come to think of it) had supposedly and painstakingly named every – single – rock. Whether that encompassed the stones on the beach, the boulders in the shipping wall and the pebbles in people's shoes was unclear; as was whether anyone would receive a response if they shouted Dolphin, Half Moon, Hedgehog or Coffin Box at the local geography. Next time you're in the area, I urge you to try it.

With only a few hours of daylight left, Madelyn and I decided to plunge straight into the heart of Cádiz where there was no mistaking we were in the Old Town. Multiple buildings were in the process of receiving a major facelift; their weathered façades shedding layers of pink paint like a second skin. Floral pots, dripping with remnants of recent hydration, swung daintily from well-loved balconies. Vespas of varying colours and designs were parked on every corner, waiting patiently for their owners to employ them. Unlike on the hill we'd sauntered up earlier, the entire community was outside enjoying the sunshine as the locals swept pavements and chatted animatedly to one another from their doorsteps.

That was the beauty of Cádiz. It may have felt like an enormous sprawling metropolis, but the majority of the population was actually squished into a narrow grid of about 4.5 square kilometres. No wonder David Palomar once said he'd never seen so much talent about the place. With an average of 30,000 people crammed into every square kilometre, the odds of finding someone *fenomenal* were pretty high (unless you lived on a hill or drove a truck).

Down an endlessly charming laneway, Madelyn and I happened upon a flamenco dance school where a certain suave singer may well have begun his career.

And then we saw him.

David Palomar.

He was at the end of an alleyway, looking gloriously towards the sky.

There was no mistaking it was him because the words "David Palomar" were emblazoned underneath him. Okay, so it wasn't actually *physically* him but more a *poster* of him promoting the upcoming album launch he'd so kindly messaged me about. But it was close enough.

I had to get a photo. Unfortunately, a chain-smoking, tracksuit-wearing old lady was standing beside the poster, staring back at me as much as her cataracts would allow. For all I knew, she could have been David's aunt or one of his loyal groupies who painstakingly devoted themselves to guarding his images from unwanted Australian advances. Had I opted for an extreme close-up, I still would have had to stand directly in front of her. To throw Her Wrinkled Highness off the scent, I walked a couple of steps away, pirouetted, then took the fastest picture of my life. I managed to capture both the bemused old biddy and David's likeness in the one frame. It ended up being one of my favourite photos from the trip.

Before we returned to Seville, Madelyn and I earnestly retraced our steps back to the ceramic tile shop but there was still no sign of the shopkeepers.

'Bloody hell.' Madelyn was not amused.

'Bloody hell!' I echoed when we descended to sea level. A huge protest was underway right outside the entrance to the train station where a colossal crowd of disgruntled workers were yelling and waving placards about. 'At least we know where the owners of the tile shop got to,' I whispered as scores of ridiculously good-looking riot police stood on the fringes surveying the scene. Without wanting to get caught up in all the chaos, Madelyn and I found a side entrance and snuck into the station.

Fortunately, the 6 p.m. train to Jerez was right on schedule – it just turned out to be the wrong train; a miscalculation we discovered about 15 minutes into our journey when a guard came by to check our tickets. The only way we were ever going to see Jerez again, he patiently explained, was if we changed trains at the balmy-sounding Bahía Sur – or South Bay Station – that turned out to be anything but.

When Madelyn and I stepped onto its desolate platform, frozen winds blasted through our flimsy coats like icy darts and, with nowhere to shelter from the blistering conditions (or any idea of when the next train would arrive), we sat on a frosty stone bench and huddled together for dear life. A rather foreboding-looking penitentiary, surrounded by barbed wire and illuminated with stadium lights, leered at us from the other side of the tracks.

'Geez, I wouldn't want to end up in there.' I groaned as my teeth chattered in the wind.

'What, the shopping centre?' asked Madelyn.

I rubbed the icicles from my eyes. Sure enough, right beside the prison was a dichotomously cheery sign for the local supermarket.

'I guess if the locals are ever busted for pickpocketing, they don't have far to go to be incarcerated,' I joked. It sure gave new meaning to the word convenience.

It was a shame I'd never heard of classical flamenco dancer and choreographer Antonio Ruiz Soler. Apart from Pablo Picasso personally autographing the bottom of his swimming pool once, one of Antonio's most important legacies – other than appearing in Hollywood movies in the 1940s – was adapting flamenco songs for dance; Ángel's powerful *martinete* being one of them. Without Señor Soler's influence, I may never have returned to Spain.

To honour the *legendario* Antonio (who had sadly passed away), another dancer – also by the name of Antonio – was dedicating an entire show to the original Antonio in the imaginatively titled spectacular: *Antonio*. The only downside was the earlier Antonio used to infuse flamenco with ballet and folk dancing. That meant I could either spend two hours watching a potentially castanet-wielding man in tights jump about, or I could take advantage of the landlords having gone away and catch a late-night *siesta* before I joined everyone at the bar afterwards. There was no choice, really.

The likelihood of any peace and quiet was quickly shot to pieces when the landlords decided to delay their departure by a day – unless Gabriela's idea of a vacation was to stay home, crank up the idiot box and get her husband and dog to clomp around in her stilettos all evening. Not to be outdone, Markus – who had also skipped Antonio's show – used the spare time to practise footwork on the tiles beside my bedroom.

'Staaace!' Madelyn greeted me with a sherry at the bar afterwards. 'You missed out big time, girl!'

'Was it a good show?' I asked hesitantly.

'Not only was it a great performance, but Antonio danced with his shirt off!'

'Seriously?!'

'He's your type too.'

'You mean he had boofy hair?!'

'The works.'

Excelente.

'Eh-Stacey!' Vicente shouted from across the bar. He dispensed a huge hug before pushing a generous plate of *tortilla* into my hands. '*No trigo.*' He winked. Sebastian then appeared by my side and informed me that earlier that day, Vicente had driven 150 kilometres – *¡150 kilómetros!* – to pick wild, white asparagus that he'd baked into two giant *tortillas* for us to enjoy.

There was an interesting saying about asparagus in Spain: '*Los espárragos de abril para mí, los de mayo para el amo, y los de junio para ninguno (o el burro)*' which roughly meant: 'April's asparagus is the best for me, May's are for the master and June's are for no one (unless you're a donkey)'. With no mention of the month of March, I assumed its asparagus was the best parting gift for Australians.

'Vicente!! This is *muy delicioso*!' I beamed. It was the most divine *tortilla* I had ever eaten, infused with the most essential ingredient of all – Vicente's love.

Just when the night couldn't get any better, the *maestro* Manolo Marín walked into the bar. Within seconds, he recognised Sebastian from Seville and asked if he could join our table. We were so honoured, we lavished him with free drinks and much of Vicente's bounty. Manolo had been fortunate enough to witness flamenco's glorious evolution for decades and, as the living encyclopedia of a man generously shared stories with us about its vibrant history and inspirations, we enthusiastically hung off his every word. (Fortunately, since the only sketchy Spanish I knew related to flamenco, I didn't have to ask for a translation every five seconds.)

Afterwards, when Vicente and Manolo fell into a deep conversation, I perched up at the bar alongside one of the nicer German girls from class who had some very grave news to impart. She and her fellow *compatriotas* were due to fly back to Germany the following morning and would miss Blanca's final lesson. Not only would my *mantón* and I have oodles of space, I wouldn't have to worry about anyone pinching my spot again.

'Oh, that's too bad.' I feigned dismay.

'Blanca's teaching has been a revelation, don't you think?'

'Definitely,' I agreed without hesitation.

'She's so generous with her knowledge and wisdom. Who else would teach you so many different versions of a dance?' I certainly couldn't think of anyone. Suddenly, the melancholic *Mädchen* became even more serious. 'Please.' She looked me straight in the eye. 'Whatever you do in the last class tomorrow, treat it as art. Get out of your head and improvise from your heart.' As bumper sticker-sounding as her challenge was, she'd made an excellent point. What was the point of doing *anything* in life if you didn't throw caution to the wind and completely embrace each and every experience?

Our meaningful exchange was interrupted by an intoxicated man breaking into a mournful lament. Everyone in the bar immediately fell into a respectful silence and offered hushed *jaleos* for his gut-wrenching grief. The singer deeply articulated the sorrow I felt at having to say goodbye to Vicente (that, and the fact that we'd just run out of *tortilla*).

32

ADIÓS POR AHORA
Ciao for Now

When in Spain, it was all very well to splash out on flouncy new flamenco apparel but when your backpack was already pushing the 25-kilogram luggage limit, there were only two ways of getting everything home: wear every single item of flamenco clothing back on your international flight, or find a way to ship them direct to your house. The fact that I couldn't even breathe whilst sitting in my slinky, black-and-white *sevillana* skirt cemented my decision for the latter.

Naturally, Madelyn wanted in and, within minutes, had managed to procure a jumbo-sized cardboard box into which we stuffed all of our recently acquired shawls, skirts, dresses and fans. Word on the flamenco grapevine was that you could ship anything anywhere from Spain using cash on delivery. Since I couldn't pronounce half the phrases that related to the Spanish postal system in my guidebook, I texted Simone for backup.

'*I'll meet you at the post office as soon as I can!*' she replied.

Lugging a heavy box of flamenco treasures up a steep hill wasn't as fun as we thought it would be and when Madelyn and I eventually found the central post office, Simone was yet to materialise – nothing to do with the extraordinarily short notice I'd given her, I was sure.

'Blanca's class starts pretty soon, Stace,' Madelyn reasoned. 'We probably should have organised this for this arvo.'

'What should we do then?' I shrugged. 'Wait for Sim and be late? Or come back after class?'

'Why don't you have a go?' Madelyn gestured towards the counter. Her *optimismo* was astounding.

With guidebook in hand, I took a deep breath and marched up to the counter. '*Quisiera enviar un paquete internacional a Australia. Efectivo a la entrega, por favor.*' As momentous memorised speeches went, it was certainly up there.

'*No,*' came the post office lady's unambiguous response.

'*Perdón?*'

'*No efectivo a la entrega.*' No cash on delivery.

'Oh.'

'*Se paga ahora o no se envía.*' Pay now or forget about it.

I crept over to Madelyn. 'How much cash do you have?'

'Sorry, Stace, I've got nothing on me, or in my account, until I get some transferred.'

Sighing, I whipped out my one and only card but the postal worker was having none of it. '*No hay crédito. Solamente efectivo.*'

With the Spanish postal department refusing to accept any kind of plastic currency, I raced to the nearest ATM and withdrew the last of my dwindling funds. The second I'd paid for the postage, Simone appeared.

Six weeks later, a tatty box that may have participated in the Running of the Bulls along the way – held together by the flimsiest threads of cardboard and tape – was dumped at Madelyn's front door. If it weren't for the plethora of environmentally unfriendly plastic bags we'd wrapped our precious possessions in, I'm not sure they would have lasted the distance.

Back at the dance studio, most of the students had resurfaced for Blanca's final lesson – minus most of the German contingent who were winging their way back home – and Madelyn, who had rapidly lost any of her recently acquired mojo. In her absence, I'd rehearsed a phrase to collect her certificate on her behalf.

Blanca couldn't wait until the end of the workshop to present our awards and, before we'd even warmed up, she began calling out the students' names. When I heard 'Eh-Stacey', I stepped forward and graciously accepted my award, posing much less like a demented fruitcake than I had with Ángel. Madelyn's was the last name to be read out.

'*Excusi.*' I stepped forward. '*Mi amiga tiene un resfriado.*' The room fell so silent, you could have heard a *peineta* drop. I cleared my throat and repeated the phrase, which caused everyone to look at me like *I* was the one on medication. With no one willing, or able, to decipher my incoherent ramblings, Blanca put the remaining certificates away and began the lesson.

'*Ai ai aieeeeeeeeeeeeeeeeeeeeeeeeeeeeeeeee,*' wailed the singer; her torment fast becoming my own.

BOOM! Diddli-boom, strum, DONG, diddli-TWANG!! The guitarist's opening chords were so thunderous, passing pedestrians could have sworn the building was being detonated. I couldn't take another second.

'*Por favor, es demasiado!!*' I pleaded with the guitarist. He looked puzzled but continued to play, most likely because he couldn't freaking hear a word I had said. '*Por favor, por favor!*' I tried a different tactic and pointed from the microphone to the speakers before covering my ears. Immediately, the guitarist stopped playing. I may have had his *atención*, but I still didn't have his *comprensión*. Blanca then stopped the lesson and, along with the rest of the students, stared incredulously at me. Once again, I pointed to the speakers and cringed (but in hindsight, it probably just looked like I didn't like his playing).

In the end, it took two Germans (who must have missed the plane), one French girl and the rest of the European subcontinent to interpret what I was saying. When clarity prevailed, Blanca immediately marched over and yanked the microphone away from the guitarist as another student pushed the speakers further back. Blanca then gestured for me to stand on the opposite side of the studio, well away from the musicians. I was so grateful, I inundated her with '*Muchísimas gracias*'.

'*De nada.*' She smiled. What a woman.

In honour of our last class, and the half-hearted promise I'd made to the German girl at the bar, I threw myself with reckless abandon into the final component of the dance – the *bulería* – during which the students and I laughed and scurried around as we gleefully tried to capture Blanca's ever-changing choreography.

Before the final group photo, Blanca read out the last of the names on the certificates. When Madelyn was called, once again, I stepped forward and was only able to announce, '*Esa es mi amiga*,' before the entire class burst into applause, assuming I had somehow become Madelyn. Before I could correct them, I was ushered into Blanca's waiting arms for more hugs, congratulations and yet another photo. In a class of only 15 remaining pupils, somehow not one of them had noticed that the only inept, sensitive-eared, amateur mime artist amongst them had received her certificate twice. *Bravo.*

Before I left, I wanted to make peace with the guitarist and assure him not all Australians possessed such supersonic hearing. The moment I told him where I was from his face lit up and, in broken English, he told me he'd lived in Sydney once (*¡Qué bonito!*), but still couldn't get over the fact that it took around 30 hours to fly between the two countries (*¡Dios mío!*). After a lilting conversation peppered with nods, smiles and laughs, we parted as firm friends.

For the final Teatro spectacular, the who's who of flamenco had assembled to pay tribute to world-renowned choreographer and dancer Mario Maya. Mario's daughter Belén, a famous dancer in her own right, had not only put the production together, but had managed to persuade Manuel Betanzos from Seville – who rarely performed live anymore – to join the lineup. Belén was restaging 10 of her father's dramatic choreographies that were to feature as many of Mario's former students, in as many of the original – but freshly laundered – costumes, as possible.

As far as Mario had been concerned, rules were made to be broken and, for the first surprise of the evening, a male dancer performed an *alegría* – the happy dance I'd only ever seen women showcase before. Then, just a week after she set the stage alight in her solo show, Isabel Bayón returned with a blistering *jaleo*. Next up, Manuel Betanzos, dressed as a bullfighting *torero*, danced perfectly in unison with four other male dancers, followed by a recreation from Carlos Saura's film *Flamenco*. Understandably, the most moving tribute of all was performed by Belén Maya herself, where the recent grief of her father's passing was achingly evident in her intensely heartfelt *seguiriya*.

Unfortunately, with lots of sherry in my belly, there was no way I was going to make it to the finale without making a quick pit stop and when I jumped up from my retractable seat, a cavernous KABOOM echoed throughout the theatre. With the entire audience suddenly aware of my idealistic intentions, I fell into a blind panic and stumbled over several pairs of legs on the way out the *auditorio*.

Unsurprisingly, there wasn't a scrap of toilet paper to be found in the first cubicle, so I flung myself into the second stall, but failed to notice a large puddle of water that caused me to slip and crash spectacularly into the wall with an almighty THUD. When I finally returned to the theatre all bruised and battered, I couldn't for the life of me find my allocated seat and spent some other famous dancer's entire solo manhandling my way back to safety.

I arrived back just in time to witness the dramatic climax – another theatrical tribute to Lorca, but with a much darker tone that involved an evil, dreadlocked, Mad Max-looking character who, instead of dancing, pestered some poor sod in a menacingly bizarre scene reminiscent of *Beetlejuice*. Frankly, I'd had more fun falling over in the bathroom.

When the house lights finally flickered back on, they illuminated a figure filming in the background. 'Felipe?!' I called out. The cameraman looked around to see who had recognised him. 'Felipe! It is you!' I raced over. '*Soy* Stacey! *Soy de Australia! Soy tengo* um … ah … I'm the Australian girl who phoned you about Ángel!' I puffed with exertion. 'I saw you at the café with Ángel the other day.'

'Ah jes, Eh-Stacey!' Felipe greeted me with a double kiss. 'Eet's zo nice to meet you! Have you been in Jerez ze whole time?' he asked.

'*Sí!* I learnt from Ángel last week and I just finished up with Blanca today. There's so much flamenco everywhere, I never want it to end!' I gushed.

'Bery good. We are bery happy to have you in Jerez.' Felipe grinned.

'I'd come back every year if I had the *dinero*.'

'Jes, I understand.'

'Um, Felipe.' It was now or never. 'Do you know when Paco Peña might be coming back to Australia?'

'Ah jes, later thiz year we think.'

'Oh wow, really?! And … do you know if Ángel will be in the show?'

'Oh jes and zees time, there could be some dayz off.'

'What?!' I almost knocked the poor guy over with enthusiasm alone. 'That's brilliant!'

'Eh-Stacey, let us keep in contact, jes?' Felipe requested as he began packing up his camera gear.

'Jes! I mean yes!' I handed over one of my sweaty business cards. '*Gracias*, Felipe! *Encantada*.'

'*Ciao*, Eh-Stacey. Nice to meet you too. I hope we zee you again zoon.' Felipe kissed me goodbye.

I was officially in. Nothing could spoil my *euforia*: not a lifetime of imminent construction noise, nor even an orchard filled with olives. That was, until I met Alexandra – a dancer friend of Sebastian's who'd recently arrived from Russia. Sebastian was kindly showing her the sights of Jerez before she commenced classes the following week.

To celebrate our last evening together, Sebastian invited Madelyn, Markus and me to join him and Alexandra at Jerez's oldest *peña*, but Madelyn had yet to pack and procrastinate over actually doing any university study for once, and Markus had already made alternate plans. It would have been *demente* of me to decline, considering I'd missed almost a month's worth of nocturnal adventures already.

'Goodbye, Markus! Thanks so much for everything!' Sebastian, Madelyn and I bade our tall friend a fond farewell. 'See you next year!'

'It's been an absolute pleasure, everyone. Safe travels and *hasta la próxima!*' Markus grinned. Madelyn was next to fly the coop and, after exchanging a heartfelt goodbye with Sebastian, only the three of us remained.

It was just a matter of time.

'Are we going to the same *peña* tonight?' I asked Sebastian as we trudged our way through yet another tangle of tree-lined alleyways.

'Nah, Stace. Tonight we're off to the Peña Flamenca Los Cernícalos.'

'Sounds fancy.'

By the time we reached the club, a sizeable crowd had gathered outside. When the wooden doors were eventually flung open, it was impossible not to get swept up in the excitement of it all, unless your name was Alexandra. After somehow managing to clinch three seats together near the front row, Sebastian wisely positioned himself in the middle to act as both interpreter (Alexandra spoke only Russian and Spanish) and peacemaker – Alexandra was extra surly, Sebastian explained, as she'd just broken up with her girlfriend. I would have hated to have seen her on a good day.

With Sebastian permanently based overseas, it was going to be our last catch-up for a very long time and we wasted no time gasbagging like a couple of old biddies before the show, reminiscing fondly on our shared flamenco journey thus far. Naturally, our behaviour annoyed the glowering Ms. Russia no end and she blew up and angrily berated Sebastian (in Spanish) for ignoring her when she'd only just arrived in his country.

If I'd known the Russian/Spanish for – 'You know what, love? I've flown here from the other side of the world and have known Sebastian a LOT longer than you. Considering you've got both him and Spain to yourself for the next month, you should suck it up, Buttercup!' – I would have let her have it but, alas, it was not to be. Instead, Sebastian and I continued to shoot the breeze, ignoring the increasingly livid lady in our midst.

On the stroke of midnight, a hot, young guitarist, two *fabuloso* singers and a *palmero* walked onto the stage and with every single one of them of the male persuasion, it was already shaping up to be a great show. After an enjoyable first act, Sebastian pointed out a local dancer by the name of Ana María López in the crowd. Ana was the reigning "Queen of the Bulería de Jerez" and, when she wasn't devoting hours of her time to teaching her beloved *palo*, you could be sure she would be dancing it somewhere.

When the handsome guitarist began strumming the opening bars of a local *bulería*, Ana bounded onto the stage and instantly endeared the audience with her cheeky, frenetic dance style. The more *jaleos* and encouragement we gave, the wilder she became. In the midst of one of her bamboozling improvisations, Ana spotted one of her Japanese students in the crowd. With no time for pleasantries, Ana literally dragged the young woman onto the stage and summoned her to dance a few *letras* for us.

The chances of flamenco royalty ever inviting a mere underling to perform in the hallowed halls of a sacred *peña* were, I assumed, intoxicatingly rare. Although the audience members and I could tell how mortified the student was, we weren't going to let her miss the opportunity of a lifetime. As we clapped, cheered and hollered our support, the young woman took a few hesitating steps into the spotlight, as the driving tempo of a feisty *bulería* pulsed through her veins.

With all eyes on her, there was no option but to take the proverbial bull by the horns and freaking go for it.

Slowly, but surely, the young dancer overcame her inhibitions and surrendered to the music, transforming from a reticent wallflower into a powerful, take-no-prisoners *bailaora* – utterly possessed by the unrelenting might of the *compás*. She was so compelling, even Alexandra looked minutely impressed.

After the gratifying show, every *aficionado* was out on the city streets celebrating the final night of the festival, including American Barbara, Australian Beth and a gaggle of remaining German biddies. At one point I swore I even saw, or more precisely *heard*, Loud Palmas Lady in the mix.

'So this is it, hey Stace?' Sebastian put his arms around me.

'Take care, *guapo*. It was so good to see you again.' I reluctantly gave my friend the biggest hug I could muster. 'Keep following your dreams, Seb. I'm so proud of you.'

Alexandra? Not so much.

In a giddy haze of wonder and lament, I stood silent for several moments and soaked up the last of my adventures in Andalucía, reflecting upon a treasured month of flamenco *memorias*. '*Muchas gracias,*' I whispered to the intoxicating Spanish winds, before I floated back to the apartment on a sea of satiety, and the occasional squished orange.

33

REMATE
End of an Era

It was all very strange. There wasn't a sliver of noise to be heard throughout the apartment complex – not a single hammer, stiletto, barking dog, dance rehearsal or badly dubbed telemovie. It was the most peaceful Spanish slumber that could ever have been achieved, if only my intrusive alarm clock hadn't shattered the *tranquilidad*.

'*Churros*, Stace! I gotta get one last hit!' Madelyn cried out from her apartment, flustered from yet another last-minute packing frenzy. With Simone seconding the notion via text, we organised to meet up at one of the nearby cafés where the girls could indulge in a final hurrah.

'I'm going to miss this place.' I closed the front gate of the apartment complex behind me for the last time.

'Better than missing a plane.' Madelyn was in fine form.

When it came to the gluteny goodness of *churros*, I'd only ever been a spectator up until that point but there was only so many times I could watch someone dip golden, sugar-encrusted, deep-fried chunks of dough into rich, steamy, velvety hot chocolate before I cracked. Before Simone or Madelyn could say cross-contamination, I'd unpeeled a banana from my emergency stash and dipped it into the communal cup of sweet, dark amber before me. As I succumbed to its saucy embrace, beads of gooey chocolate escaped from my mouth and dripped all over my hands. Unfortunately, the wayward chocolate also dribbled all over my shirt, inadvertently encouraging me to save some for later.

'*¡Adiós, amiga!*' We hugged Simone goodbye. 'See you back in Brisbane very soon!'

'*Hasta pronto*, ladies! Enjoy your last couple of days in Spain!'

'*¡Adiós*, hot male torso roundabout!' I sang out as Madelyn and I trudged our way down to the train station with weighty backpacks that had been barely lightened by our recent visit to the post office. Honestly, where was Sebastian when you needed him?! When Madelyn and I arrived at the station, I was delighted to discover the return ticket I'd bought in Seville had expired the previous day, forcing me to join the mounting queue of exhausted students at the ticketing office with the same dilemma.

The most Madelyn had ever seen of Seville was the interior of the Santa Justa train station and I was eager to show her there was a little more to the charming city than that. I had missed

Seville acutely and was thrilled to have one last opportunity to misplace myself – and Madelyn – in its memorable midst.

After we stuffed our backpacks into one of the lockers at Santa Justa, it took us only three-quarters of an hour to locate the correct bus into town. Then, once in the heart of Seville, we unabashedly hit the tourist trail, determined to purchase as many tacky, last-minute souvenirs as common decency – and our luggage – would allow. Sadly, none of the frilly shawl-wearing, polka-dotted, Carnaval-looking flamenco dolls I happened upon were anything like my original, but there were so many other tawdry trinkets available (bull's head shaped-slippers and flamenco dancer-shaped cheese graters) that it was easy to get distracted.

After a spot of aimless wandering, a spectacular mirage suddenly emerged from the urban ashes. Rumours had swirled about the mythical behemoth for centuries (well, probably just since it had been built), but in all my time in Seville, I'd never managed to find it, let alone known its name to seek directions to it. It was THE biggest, busiest *tapas* bar you could ever spend eternity imagining and, before I could shout, 'Gee, this place looks a little pricey!', Madelyn had found us a couple of seats by the bar.

'Sherry or red wine?' Madelyn bellowed over the pumping Spanish pop music and animated chatter of the mostly young clientele.

'Bugger that, let's having *sangría*!' I hollered back. I'd been in the land of *fiestas* for 32 days and had yet to sample an authentic glass of my favourite beverage of all time (trust me, the cask version didn't count). '*Dos sangrías, por favor!*' I signalled to the bartender. '*Con vino tinto!*' I added hastily. I refused to wrap my lips around a *sangría blanca*, or white *sangría* – a complete waste of white wine as far I was concerned. *Sangre* meant blood and, in my haughty opinion, its alcoholic namesake should only ever be made with a full-bodied blushing red so robust, it could strip varnish off a chair at 10 paces. Whilst I could still hold focus, I ordered the one dish I knew would complete the culinary equivalent of bliss. '*Quiero patatas alioli, por favor!*' I cried.

Plonk. A generous serving of plump potato cubes smothered in a rich, creamy garlic sauce was placed on the bar before us, alongside two tall glasses filled with ferociously fruity aromas.

'*¡Salud!*' I raised my glass to Madelyn.

'Bloody amen to that,' she concurred.

Clink.

Everything was better when you were inebriated. As we waited at the bus stop for a half-hourly bus that came only hourly, Madelyn and I had no clue as to whether we were even catching the correct coach in the right direction, let alone where to disembark. In spite of our best efforts, we reunited with our backpacks and found our way to the airport.

What would you do if you had an hour to kill before a flight? Try and soak up all the alcohol you'd just consumed so you didn't get kicked off the plane was one idea that sprung to mind. A slice of buttery *tortilla* and a gluten-free chocolate pastry rounded off my carb-laden binge for the day – highlights of which had included a breakfast omelette with rice and some of Madelyn's *patatas fritas* from McDonald's.

There was no way my rebellious jeans would try to weasel their way off my backside on public transport anymore. I was so full, by the time Madelyn and I boarded the plane to Barcelona, even a thick slice of "poopy seed bread" from the in-flight menu did not appeal.

Due to my tall tales of airport delinquency, Madelyn was so paranoid about being pickpocketed when we arrived in Barcelona, she wanted to sew all of her money into her knickers. I'd come up with an even more cunning plan: that of putting a disgustingly rude note in my jacket pocket in the hopes that any potential thieves would not only have been able to decipher my scratchy chicken scrawl, but would have understood enough eloquent, expletive-ridden Spanglish to have left me alone.

As Madelyn and I disembarked onto the tarmac, we assumed our best "don't mess with us" flamenco faces, but our ambitions were all in vain. There was hardly a soul at the terminal. All the airport pickpockets must have been on *siesta*; a fun fact I inadvertently discovered when I retrieved what I thought was a map from my jacket pocket to help a fellow tourist with directions later that evening. *¡¡#@$%!!*

'What's the name of our hotel again, Stace?' Madelyn asked as we hopped on the city-bound train. With two days of sightseeing up our sleeves, I had booked us into Barcelona's most elusive *pensión*. One would think after all the palaver of misplacing it the first time around, I may have paid a little more attention on my return, but it was not to be. Although Madelyn and I managed to disembark at the correct train station, we still spent the next hour painstakingly and authentically recreating almost my original journey from scratch. It was 11:30 p.m. before the *pensión's* never-ending flight of stairs finally emerged.

Once we were settled into our surprisingly spacious double room, I was excited to take Madelyn to the bustling, standing-room-only *tapas* bar I hadn't had the chutzpah to enter the first time around, but since it was a Sunday, every single eating establishment – including the homely Irish pub and the trusty old pork-and-poodle parlour – was closed. The only outlet still serving food was a cute little hole-in-the-wall café and although its kitchen had closed for the evening, the waiter kindly offered us a selection of cold, pre-plated *tapas*.

With weary eyes and eager stomachs, Madelyn and I gratefully supped on juicy champignons and slices of thick aubergine *tortilla*, washed down with a couple of glasses of hearty red wine. Having David Bowie blaring in the background certainly enlivened proceedings somewhat, as did the jokes about gluten the waiter made every time I went to take a bite out of anything.

I really was going to miss the place.

34

EN EL CAMINO CONTRATIEMPO
On the Offbeaten Track

Shafts of light poured into the sixth floor window. I had a feeling we'd missed something. That was right – the day.

'It's 9:30 a.m.!!! For God's sake, Stace! We gotta get moving!!' Madelyn shrieked.

I flung off my eye mask and recoiled from the sun's blinding rays. 'We should have set an alarm!' I exclaimed.

'No point. You were snoring so loudly, we wouldn't have heard it!'

'Excuse me?!'

'You snored, Stace! All … night … long,' Madelyn declared.

'I snore?!' I shot back incredulously.

'Yes, you do! You sounded like a foghorn all bloody night, thank you very much.'

'Oh geez sorry, Mads. You should have woken me up!'

'I tried! I threw my pillow at you a few times but it didn't make any difference.'

That was the thing about being perpetually single. You had no idea whether you sleepwalked, sleeptalked or did Elvis impersonations all evening. Either I had unintentionally stored up a lifetime's worth of eccentricities to be unleashed upon my next unsuspecting roommate, or it was my fatigued brain's way of catching up on all the oxygen deprivation it had suffered from four consecutive weeks of less than five hours sleep a night.

Only a hop, skip and *paseo* from the *pensión* was the sprawling, tree-lined pedestrian strip known as La Rambla. Trust me, if you hadn't been pickpocketed at the airport on the way in, you could more than make up for it at Barcelona's most infamous mall. Ten years prior, when I had first visited the lengthy promenade, it had been crawling with tourists, vendors and thieves. When Madelyn and I rocked up, however, the precinct was only mildly occupied with a disproportionate number of frozen statue street performers (whom, we assumed, were really pickpockets in disguise).

Halfway up the kilometre-long boulevard, we finally discovered where everyone was at: the Mercat de Sant Josep de la Boqueria. Forget everything you had ever seen or heard about any marketplace anywhere on the planet – La Boqueria was the Mother of all Markets. To prove the point, it had even been awarded World's Best Food Market once. It sounded like love at first bite.

Aisles and miles of fresh fruits, nuts, cheeses, mushrooms, eggs, herbs, seafood, poultry, abhorrent olives, breads, preserves, biscuits, pastries, charcuterie, pastas, wines and candied fruits overwhelmed our olfactories at every turn.

In the snack section alone there was literally a wall of confectionary – an enormous, heaving patchwork filled with every shape, size and colour of sweet ever made. Shoppers were falling into diabetic comas just strolling past.

At yet another stand was a display of cups filled with the most beautiful pastel pinks, creams, ambers and oranges courtesy of luscious juice combinations like coconut and papaya, strawberry and pineapple, mango and berry. A decadently creamy coconut and strawberry juice soon had me in conniptions and, if it wasn't Madelyn's first visit to Barcelona, I would have contentedly remained at La Boqueria for the rest of my life.

You couldn't throw a fake baby in Barcelona without hitting the architectural works of one Antoni Gaudí. Scattered throughout the city were cathedrals, apartment buildings and public parks illumined by his unique designs and, for a limited time only, the central El Corte Inglés store was showcasing a Gaudí exhibit that Madelyn was keen to see but, much like our secretive *pensión*, half the fun was actually finding it.

'Where the bloody hell is it?!' Madelyn bellowed on our third expedition up the department store's escalators. For 15 minutes we had been dutifully following the signs dotted throughout the retail giant's haberdashery and homeware departments, but were yet to find anything too gaudy.

'*Arriba. Está arriba!*' the staff kept informing us.

'We've been bloody *arriba*! We can't get any more *arriba*!' Madelyn insisted before turning to me. '*Arriba* means up, right?'

I nodded, distracted by a display of soccer ball-shaped Cheetos.

'I swear to you, Stace, we're going to find this bloody exhibit if it kills us and we're going to bloody love it!' In the end, only one of those declarations came true.

For me, buildings were like clothes. I liked them vivacious and colourful. Adorning any exterior with dreary greys or drab pastels was like living life through beige-coloured glasses. If I was given creative control, I'd paint towns all over the planet not just red, but blindingly bright with dazzling yellow, rosy pink and warm orange façades, where it would be impossible to be *miserable* amongst such kaleidoscopic magnificence.

'Hey, Mads, wait until you see La Predrera! It's my favourite Gaudí design by far,' I enthused. It was only when we reached La Predrera that I realised I had the wrong name for it. The apartment complex I'd been besotted with since I first laid eyes on it 10 years prior was called Casa Milà. Sure, Gaudí's gothic-inspired La Predrera was spectacular with its soft, grey undulating walls and flowing curved balconies, but it was no Casa Milà.

When Madelyn and I schlepped over to where my all-time favourite building was *supposed* to be, there was no sign of it anywhere, not even hidden behind any scaffolding. I hoped someone from the nearby Starbucks could shed some light on the matter, but the young server behind the counter had no clue as to its whereabouts – mostly because I had inadvertently asked her where *mi casa* was as opposed to Casa Milà. Fortunately for her, she hadn't known where I lived, otherwise I would have had her up on charges.

Then, quite by accident, Madelyn and I spotted Casa Milà behind some construction barriers on the opposite side of the street. I was so elated to have finally found the correct building that I was forced to overlook the fact that I still had the wrong name for it. Casa Milà was the official title for La Predrera – the grey, gothic apartment building we'd just come from.

Casa Battló turned out to be the name of the dreamy apartment complex I'd long been smitten with and I was happy to note the sentiment still abounded. The colourful creation was like a mythical sandcastle with shimmering roof shingles that resembled scales on a dragon's back. My favourite features, however, were the *Phantom of the Opera* mask-shaped balconies. Whenever I gazed upon them, I had visions of Josep Battló – the businessman whom Gaudí designed the complex for a century ago – swanning about the candlelit interior in a cape, clutching a monkey-shaped music box. Madelyn and I never found out if the building also boasted an underground lake and cathedral due to its exorbitant entrance fees, but at least Casa Battló had been completed.

The same couldn't be said for Gaudí's most famous project – La Sagrada Família – that has been under construction since the late 1800s. Since its inception, this giant, gothic art nouveau basilica has aspired to be the world's tallest religious building and was a labour of love for the highly devout Gaudí who, towards the end of his life, lived like a monk, followed a strict vegetarian diet and never married. I prayed I was not on the same path. I was an ardent believer that both mung beans and monogamy could coexist.

Tragically, one day when Gaudí was either on his way to confession, to La Sagrada Família, or both, he was hit by a tram. It didn't help that he looked like a bit of a raggedy hobo at the time (yet another thing we had in common), nor that he lost consciousness after the tram ploughed into him. Had he been able to identify himself as one of the greatest architectural designers of all time – rather than a tatty street bum – medical attention may have been more forthcoming. Sadly, by the time Gaudí was recognised, it was too late and he died shortly thereafter aged 73 with the construction of his adored La Sagrada Família only a quarter of the way through.

(Whilst assembly continues at a whirring pace so, too, does a campaign to beatify the pious Gaudí. Whether he ever achieves sainthood or not, I personally believe he has already been bestowed the highest honour possible when, in 1993, his life was made into a live stage spectacular entitled *Gaudí the Musical*.)

By the time Madelyn and I left the basilica, it had been about two hours since I'd ingested a potato of any kind (unless you counted the Cheetos) and I was chomping at the bit for another hit. Somehow, amidst the glitz and glamour of Gucci and Armani outlets, Madelyn found a deserted *tapas* bar that looked like it was straight out of *Seinfeld*. After ordering my heart's desire in flawed Spanish, the barman responded in flawless English and, not long after, Madelyn and I found ourselves up to our elbows in the naughtiest *patatas alioli* yet – with dollops of fatty mayonnaise so globular and congealed, they refused to mingle with any of the deep-fried cubes of carbs below.

'Hey, watch it!'

'Ouch, be careful!'

It was peak hour at Passeig de Gràcia. A flurry of tourists and commuters, all hell-bent on getting somewhere faster than the other, pushed and shoved at us from every angle, *inconsciente* to the *caos* they were causing. Madelyn and I soon became separated in the hubbub and, as she was pushed towards the oncoming train, someone pressed down hard on her right foot. When she turned to glare at the offender, a sneaky little hand appeared on her left, trying to gain access into her handbag.

'Stace!' Madelyn cried out. 'Someone's just tried to grab my purse!'

'What!?! Did you see who it was?' I shrieked as we squeezed into the only compartment of space left on the carriage.

'That's her!' Madelyn pointed to a scraggly, blonde-haired woman in an unironed shirt and slacks, standing only a couple of metres away from us. Two young children clung shyly to her side.

'That whole family just tried to pickpocket you?!' I

asked incredulously, trying to ignore the alarming fact that the thieves and I shared the same fashion sense (which was probably why I hadn't been targeted of late).

'One of them stood on me and the other tried to slip their hand into my bag!'

'We should take a photo of them! Show it to the police!' I proclaimed.

'What are they going to do, Stace? Half the bloody population steals.'

'But you caught them in the act! They're standing right there!'

Unsurprisingly, the ragtag family avoided our steely gaze and Madelyn and I watched helplessly as they disembarked at the following station. If the family had its sights set on the airport, they would need a lot more practise.

PARK GÜELL 1250m.

It was a sign.

Not only that, it was pointing us to Gaudí's most scenic open-air attraction, perched high in the hills above Barcelona. I tucked my tiny tourist map away, relieved I wouldn't have to try and navigate anymore.

'The sign says it's this way, honey, but our map says it's this way.' A middle-aged American couple were in deep discussion by the pedestrian crossing outside Lesseps station.

'Are you looking for Gaudí's Park?' Madelyn enquired.

'Yes, we are.'

'It's straight up this road.'

'Yes, but the map says to go along to the right first,' the husband disputed.

'Nope, it's this way, straight up the hill. That's what the sign says. You can follow us if you like,' Madelyn offered and, with those fateful words, we were off.

'Where are you both from?' I asked as we trudged up the incline.

'Minnesota,' came the reply.

'Ah.' All I knew of Minnesota was that people had weird accents, it was supersonically cold and yet, despite all of that, Prince had always lived there.

Halfway up the first never-ending hill, we ran into a young couple on the same mission. Four soon became six, but no one bothered to ask where they were from in order to preserve vital oxygen.

After a good 20 minutes of trekking up a slope so steep our noses were pressed against the bitumen, I began to get a little skeptical.

'Hey, Mads, I'm sure it didn't take me this long to find the park last time.'

'Your tour bus probably dropped you off at the main entrance. Come on, Stace. We're almost there.'

'It just doesn't feel like the right way.'

'Quit your whinging woman and walk!'

Not long after, the young couple suddenly turned on their heels and took off to the right, abandoning us without another thought.

'They're crazy,' Madelyn declared as we marched further up the offending rise. When the four of us reached a kind of plateau, we stopped to make sense of our surroundings.

'This isn't it, Mads,' I confirmed.

'Well, where's the sign then?'

'Hang on, what does your map say?' I asked as I pulled mine from my back pocket.

'I've only got one for the metro.'

'It still looks like it's off to the right,' Minnesotan Man reiterated as we huddled around his crinkled map.

'What a sec, what's that?' I exclaimed, pointing up an adjoining hill. 'That's the park entrance! I'm sure of it!' No one needed to be told twice. Off we traipsed, through a gully of apartment buildings, towards what we hoped were the pearly gates of Güell – that turned out to be the entrance to someone's private property instead.

'Ah geez sorry, everyone. A lot can change in a decade,' I ventured. You could have cut the *tensión* with a *machete*. 'Look, let's just ask someone for directions. We're clearly lost.'

'Why are Gaudí's designs always so bloody hard to find?!' Madelyn fumed.

Just at that moment, a father and daughter appeared on their driveway. 'Excuse me!' Minnesotan Man shouted and raced over before they had a chance to lock themselves inside. Seconds later, he returned sporting a big grin. 'They said it's not too far from here!'

'Hurrah!' Everyone cheered.

'All we have to do is head up to the right where all that vegetation is.'

Trekking up a torturously steep slope led us to a vacant expanse of deserted scrub.

'Great park,' Madelyn muttered under her breath.

'*Perdón!*' I hurled myself at a passing jogger. '*Por favor! Hilfe!* Can you help us please? We're looking for Park Güell.'

'Zi park? Eet eez zat way. Go right, around zis hill, down ze road and zen you will zee eet.'

'*Merci!*' I shouted deliriously.

The Minnesotans had finally reached their limit and, armed with what they realised to have been the correct directions all along, they power-walked ahead of us without so much as a glance or obscene gesture. It was the last we ever saw of them.

One hour, two empty bottles of water and 18,467 hills later, Madelyn and I reached Park Güell. Unfortunately by then, so had hundreds of other tourists.

If it wasn't for a wealthy textile baron in the late 1800s, Park Güell may never have been dreamt into existence. Count Eusebi Güell was such a fan of Gaudí's work, he commissioned him to build an exclusive housing estate for the aristocracy of Barcelona to reside in (although the fact that the Count had 10 children of his own to house might have also had something to do with it). There was only one catch if you wanted to live in such a regally remote location: all dwellings had to be built according to Gaudí's strict rules of design. To entice prospective tenants, a beautiful display home was built but, when only two plots out of a possible 60 ever sold, the wildly optimistic idea was abandoned and Gaudí ended up moving into the display home with some of his family. When Count Güell kicked the bucket several years later, the land was taken over by the council and opened up to the public.

Two life-sized gingerbread cottages laden with icing-sugared roofs and candy cane chimneys were the first hint that it was to be no ordinary walk in the park. Fountains, statues, palm trees and sculptures then kept visitors enthralled as they ascended a grandiose stone stairwell into the heart of what could only be described as Spanish Disneyland. Halfway up the stairs, a considerable crowd had gathered with everyone jostling for position to be the next to get their photo taken beside a brightly coloured tile salamander. Never one to follow trends, I asked Madelyn to take a photo of me lying on the lower part of the wall with my head in a bush instead. Creativity knew no bounds.

Once at the elongated summit, Madelyn and I darted through scores of sightseers and pigeons (the latter of which were no doubt enjoying their last days of freedom before they ended up in someone's freezer), and savoured the incredibly panoramic views before us. Awash with a sea of endless buildings, stretching languidly as they dissolved into the distant haze of the sparkling azure sea, Barcelona was resplendent. I may have even spotted a couple of trees amidst the urban sprawl.

High in the craggy peaks of the Collserola Mountain range behind us, the Tibidabo Amusement Park – built around the same time as Park Güell – teetered precariously and, most alarmingly, still had most of its original attractions in operation, including a red Avió airplane ride that had been chugging along since 1928. Powered by its own propellers, the plane was a replica of the first aircraft ever to fly between Barcelona and Madrid and jutted out so far over the mountain's edge, passengers felt like they were literally flying over the city. It was a travel insurer's dream.

There was so much to explore at Park Güell but, since it had taken Madelyn and me the better part of the day to actually get there, *tiempo* was of the *esencia*. In order to find our way back to the *pensión* before nightfall, I purchased a more comprehensive map from the gift shop and stood outside surveying the best way back to the metro. Just then, one of the park's pigeons decided to leave its calling card. Although its aim was a little off – missing Lesseps station by a couple of centimetres – the gesture was appreciated.

Our descent back to the train station took just minutes. Clearly marked signs were positioned all along the route that pointed either down to the metro or back up to Park Güell, making it impossible to even dream of taking a detour.

'I don't think we'll have time to hit the beach this arvo, Stace,' Madelyn said regretfully as we hopped onto the train. Secretly, I was kind of glad. I was still getting over my encounter a decade prior.

Barcelona was one of the final stops on the hurried bus tour of Europe my fellow travellers and I had endured and, by the time we arrived at the cosmopolitan city, we were ready to stage a mutiny if we were forced to visit yet another crusty old cathedral or historical site covered in scaffolding. When our tour leader gave us the option of spending a leisurely afternoon at one of Barcelona's most popular beaches instead, we welcomed the itinerary change with open arms, if not partial nudity.

Bobbing about in the cool, refreshing waves of the Balearic Sea fast became the highlight of everyone's trip and I, too, would have found it the most blissful afternoon on record if I wasn't completely busting at the time.

'Just go in the ocean,' one of the young Aussie men from the tour group suggested, 'like I just did.' I was back on the shore in seconds. Racing up the sandy banks, I hot-footed it across an enormous plaza where one would expect to at least find a café or someone doing *sevillanas*, but there was nothing but an urban expanse of barren bitumen as far as the eye could see. That was, until off in the shimmery distance, I spotted the beckoning beacon of a lone portaloo.

Now, I've never been one for horror movies. I'm still shaken by the one and only scary film I was made to watch in primary school, but even Freddy Krueger couldn't compete with the terror lurking within the confines of the Barcelona beach portaloo, circa 1999. As I slowly opened the creaking door, I was instantly hit with a pugnaciously repugnant stench. The toilet appeared to not have been flushed since the 1970s and had continued to stack up against the odds, so to speak. It was, as they say, a little stinky. If that wasn't distressing enough, several creative, non-toilet-trained Neanderthals had bypassed the bowl completely and had relieved themselves of every kind of affliction on the floor and walls.

The entire experience may only have lasted a few seconds, but the impact was eternal. I screamed and slammed the door shut, fleeing back to the safety of the tour group where, miraculously, I no longer needed to go.

To commemorate our final evening in Spain, Madelyn and I decided to treat ourselves to a fluffy flamenco show in La Rambla at the same historic *tablao* I first visited on the Trafalgar tour. Madelyn had invited a Scandinavian student from Jerez to join us but, unfortunately, neither option ended up materialising: the Norwegian girl was no doubt still searching for her accommodation and the *tablao* was closed for the evening.

A popular sauna that masqueraded as a tourist trap of a restaurant won our custom instead.

'American?' an overzealous waiter asked as he guided us to our table.

'Nope, Aussie,' Madelyn shot back.

'Okay. Pleaze, here are ze English menoos. Vie haf zpecial tonight – *sangría y paella* for you both, lovely ladiez. Zee? Only twelve fifty euros for you both.' The waiter (who had clearly watched too many episodes of *Fawlty Towers*) pointed to the menu. At just over €6 each, it was the bargain of the century.

'*Bien.*'

'Oh before you go, is the *paella* gluten-free?' I enquired.

'Jes,' he replied a little too eagerly.

'Just checking you understand what gluten-free is? No wheat? *No trigo?*'

'Jes.'

'Okay cool. We'll have the special then.'

'Zank you, lovely ladiez.'

'Geez, it's warm in here,' Madelyn commented, dishevelling layers.

Two jugs of water later, we discovered that not only was the dinner special €12.50 *each*, but the *paella* was LOADED with gluten, forcing me to add vengeful stomach to my expanding repertoire of bodily functions.

By the time Madelyn and I arrived back at the *pensión*, some of the guests above us were holding a furniture moving party, after which time everyone got swept up in the brand new craze of "Who Can Slam Their Bedroom Door Shut The Loudest?!" In between running to the toilet with gluten guts, and trying not to breathe/snore/blink/upset Madelyn all night long, I was rather glad to be leaving.

35

SALIDA
Exit Stage Right

'*Hola*. We'd like to check in, *por favor*.' Madelyn and I handed our travel documents over to the man at the departures desk, relieved to have made it to the airport without a) being pickpocketed, and b) no longer having to endure yet another couple unapologetically pash and paw at each other on the train.

The British Airways attendant looked at us with a raised eyebrow. 'Sorry, ladies, I cannot check you in.'

'Excuse me?!'

'Oh God, what's wrong now?' Madelyn moaned.

'You're both too early.' He shrugged. 'Come back in an hour and a half please. *Gracias*.'

'An hour and a …' I began.

'Excuse me, are you Australian?' A young woman enquired from the neighbouring check-in desk.

'Yep!' Madelyn affirmed.

'Where are you both from, if you don't mind me asking?'

'Brisbane!'

'No way! Me too! I'm Jenny. Nice to meet you.' She shook our hands. 'That's my husband Gary,' she added, pointing to a ridiculously good-looking man in the cafeteria queue. Jenny and her gorgeous Irish husband were on their way back to the Land of Potatoes after holidaying in Spain.

Mental Note #4: Move to Ireland.

With nothing to do but eat, hide from pickpockets and perve on other people's partners, I decided to splurge on my last ever authentic slice of Spanish *tortilla*, served with a zingy side salad of anchovies and tuna. Although the *tortilla* turned out to be as bland and lifeless as the Barcelona international departures lounge, it did help to kill 10 minutes.

'*Lalalalalalala lalalalala lalala*,' came a female voice over the loudspeaker.

'Do you think that's important?' I asked Madelyn.

'Probably,' she replied.

'Ladiez and gentlemen, there haz been a delay. Breetesh Airwayz flight *lalalala* to London haz been delayed. *Gracias.*'

'Jesus!' Madelyn exclaimed.

To make the most of the extra 50 minutes – and to get the taste of the other *tortilla* out of my mouth – I sought out one absolutely final slice for old time's sake. In its heyday, the chunk of potato-infused omelette would have given its contemporaries a run for its money but sadly, it had well and truly passed its used-by-date and, after one bite, was relegated to the bin.

When Madelyn and I finally boarded the plane to London, I was thrown for a loop with all of the crisp British accents on board. No longer would I be required to wildly gesticulate to get my point across whilst I mumbled in a hybrid of German, Spanish and French. I was just starting to relax when I was informed by the cabin crew that there wasn't a single scrap of gluten-free food available on the entire aircraft – not even an apple. If I hadn't recently parted ways with my rancid *tortilla*, the flight attendants might have ended up wearing it.

'This is it, Mads,' I lamented, my nose pressed up against the window as I tried to ignore the gnawing pangs of hunger emanating from my belly, 'our last glimpse of Spain.'

As frustrating as she was at times (the country, not Madelyn), there was no doubt about it. I would miss her profoundly – her vibrant colour, sassy charm and blatant disregard for societal norms. I whispered a defiant promise to return and continue my flamenco/life education in the rhythmic depths of her wildly beating heart – just so long as I didn't have to ingest any more olives.

'Stace! You made it!!' Simone raced over to give me a hug at the first flamenco lesson of the term.

'So good to see you again, Sim!' I hugged her back. 'I've been counting down the days until classes started.' I looked around the almost empty studio. 'Are Evie and Mads coming too?'

'Yeah, they're just stuck in traffic like everyone else, waiting for the storm to pass. It's a good thing you got here early.'

There was a first for everything.

Just as I was fastening the buckles on my shiny new Senovillas, I heard a guitar strum on the other side of the room. I looked over in surprise to see a new class musician warming up. I first observed his strong, sturdy hands before my gaze lingered up and over his strapping broad shoulders. By the time I noticed his chiselled chin, I was feeling a little flushed. When the guitarist's soulfully luminous and intensely dark eyes met mine, I went a little weak at the knees. His name was Martin and you can guess the rest …

i

APÉNDICE – UN POCO MÁS
Appendix – A Little More

I am ecstatic to report that since the aforementioned escapades, most of my flamenco dreams have come true – the pinnacle of which was not only did I manage to snap up the only single male flamenco guitarist in Australia at the time, but together Martin and I formed our very own flamenco troupe, complete with my rotating repertoire of sparkly new costumes and shoes.

After several years of training in Seville, Sebastian made his very own flamenco dreams come true and became a full-time international teacher and performer. His proudest accomplishment to date, however, has been becoming a father and a very loving, devoted one at that.

The gregarious Uncle Vicente continued to fill his freezer with bunnies and birds, socialising and singing into the wee hours of the night and bringing the radiant light of joy, love and adventure into the hearts of everyone he met until, most tragically as this book was being finished, Vicente suffered a very serious heart attack. This was followed by several more; the last of which stole the very last breath from his beautiful soul. He will be deeply and dearly missed.

As more and more international superstars began to grace Australian shores, the number of flamenco masterclasses soon followed, led by the incomparable Manuel Betanzos himself who ended up teaching in Brisbane two years in a row. Sharon and Sebastian then managed to organise the Joaquin Phoenix-like Andrés Peña's first ever tour of Australia, where I was thrilled to finally learn from the boofy-haired *bailaor* (although I wished I had taken the opportunity to ask him about David Palomar at the time).

All in all, life was good.

Until I went jogging.

What possessed me to go jogging for the very first time in my life, on soft sand and with no shoes on no less, would forever remain a mystery but, after just a few hundred metres, I severely rolled my ankle and was given an ultimatum by several specialists: I could either keep dancing and be crippled for the rest of my life, or give up flamenco and be able to walk pain-free long-term. It was an agonising decision. How could I possibly leave the most passionately addictive, achingly soul-stirring art form I had ever encountered?! Flamenco pulsed so vibrantly in the rhythm of my veins, I even dreamt in *compás*. I wasn't ready to give it up so, defiantly, I continued dancing.

Unsurprisingly, my ankle kept rolling. When it reached the stage where I could no longer perform, my cherished new flamenco troupe was forced to disband and, shortly after, so did my association with Martin.

But when one wooden door closes, an iron-balustraded window is flung open. When I heard Paco Peña would be touring Australia again, I hounded poor Felipe for months until I was successfully able to arrange Ángel's first ever workshop down under. Dodgy ankle or not, there was no way I was going to miss the opportunity of a lifetime!

When the morning arrived to pick Ángel and his wife up from the Brisbane Airport, I was a nervous wreck. By the time I managed to extricate myself from the house, I was already pushing it time-wise. Not having either of the couple's mobile numbers, nor any way to digitally contact them, I was sweating buckets by the time I found a car park. When I sprinted into the arrivals area, I found the bewildered flamenco couple looking as abandoned as the luggage on the carousel.

Amid profuse apologies and hugs, all was quickly forgotten and forgiven (or so I hoped), and we took off to their new home for the next two nights. Sharon and her husband had very kindly offered to host Ángel and his wife at their house (since I couldn't be trusted having him in my own). I was still so freaked out that I'd managed to pull off the impossible, and that Ángel was actually in my presence, after I introduced him and his wife to Sharon's husband, I panicked and fled – even though Sharon's husband had never met them before, didn't speak a word of Spanish and was home alone until Sharon finished work that afternoon. It wasn't my finest hour.

What then transpired over the next couple of days was a truly enchanting experience. Ángel's *tangos* workshop proved so popular, students flew from interstate to attend. Madelyn and Evie were there with bells on, alongside Sebastian who was visiting Brisbane at the time. All throughout the workshop, Ángel was the epitome of charm, grace and generosity. When the weekend came to a close, he thanked each and every student for attending, for loving his culture and embracing the way of life that was flamenco.

That evening, Sharon hosted a sumptuous dinner for us all where we spent many happy hours conversing over fabulous food and endlessly flowing red wine. Before they left to rejoin the tour, Ángel and his wife took lots of photos with me where I did my best not to look like a crazy chicken in any of them.

Sadly, over the next couple of years I completely lost touch with Ángel with all of my emails mysteriously never reaching his inbox (just like Felipe's). So when Paco announced he would be touring Australia again, I immediately set about messaging Ángel but received no response. A month later, still *nada*. There was only one option left: complete and utter stealth. On the day of Paco's Brisbane show, I lurked around the stage door waiting for a certain someone to sneak out for a cigarette. When that didn't transpire, I wrote a hastily scrawled note in Spanglish and gave it to the stage manager. Within minutes, Ángel and his wife were by my side, empowering me with hugs and kisses.

'Oh your foot. It's still bad? You're still not dancing?' Ángel asked kindly. I was shocked he'd remembered my injury from the last time he was in Brisbane. His lovely wife shook her head and tut-tutted sympathetically at my demise.

'I was trying to find you on *medios sociales* last night. I did look for you!' Ángel declared earnestly. 'But with no profile or anything, you are very ...' He paused, searching for the word. 'Clean. Nothing on you.'

'*Claro!* Nothing can get me.' I grinned.

'Are you seeing the show tonight?' Ángel asked.

'*Sí!*' I replied and began clapping like a deranged lunatic.

'It doesn't hurt your foot to see. You can always watch.' Ángel laughed and pointed to my eyes.

'And listen,' I agreed, pointing to my ears. I wisely decided to leave my loins out of the equation.

'Eh-Stacey, sorry now we have to rehearse but after, we are having lunch I think. Please come see us.'

'You sure that's okay?' I asked his tour manager when they disappeared backstage. 'I don't want Ángel to get in trouble.'

'If they invited you backstage, you have the right to be there.'

'What if I walk into the wrong changing room and Paco's in there?'

'Then he'll be surprised.'

You couldn't argue with logic.

BOOM ka ka ka BOOM ... ka ka ka BOOM ... ka ka BOOM ka ka BOOM.

The pulsating rhythms of the *cajón* throbbed throughout the Concert Hall and stirred my senses to life. I could never have imagined the journey I was about to embark on all those years ago when I first encountered Ángel on that very stage, pointing directly at me.

Once again, when Ángel strutted out for his solo, there wasn't one inch of the floorboards he didn't caress or assault with his magnificent presence. Just when you thought he was going to dance one way, he'd twist and bounce off in the other direction. Whilst he was hammering out some fast footwork, Ángel slowly turned his back to the audience; his buttocks vibrating as fast as his feet. *'Arsa,'* I whispered. Alternative sides of the auditorium were then treated to a flex of one of his pecs, followed by a wink and a kiss; after which time Ángel acknowledged the sea of flustered faces before him, grateful for the thunderous *aplausos*.

During interval, friends of mine informed me there was a spare seat beside them in the front row if I wanted to join them. Were you kidding me?! As soon as I accepted their offer, however, I started to panic – what if Ángel saw me sitting there and got distracted? Or worse, what if his wife saw me checking out parts of her husband's anatomy? In the end, they were risks I was willing to take.

I managed to stay incognito until the curtain call, when the audience burst into a unanimous standing ovation. As soon as Ángel saw me in the front row, he broke into a huge smile. As the entire company took their bows, he gave me a wink and blew me a sneaky kiss. When it was Ángel's turn in the spotlight, a huge cheer filled the auditorium and, after taking a bow, Ángel winked at me again, blowing me a much more obvious kiss. After a playful *fin de fiesta*, he exited the stage, blowing me so many *besos*, I almost got pash rash.

'Boy, he really singled you out!' my friends declared afterwards.

And for that I will be forever grateful.

Just as I was finishing this book, I decided to take a romantic trip down reminiscing lane and watched *Young Guns II* for what was possibly the 251st time. However, on this occasion, I decided to watch the credits all the way through to the end to find out the name of the guitarist who had played the haunting Spanish/Mexican-sounding music throughout the sumptuous Alan Silvestri soundtrack.

His name? Ángel Romero.

I then scrolled through the credits of *Strictly Ballroom* to ascertain the name of the flamenco guitarist who'd played in the film. It was Ángel García.

My dreams had been inspired by angels.

The celestial full circle was now complete.

And it was all thanks to Emilio Estévez.

¡¡Arsa!!

LAS MENCIONES
Acknowledgements

Muchas gracias to you, the reader, for purchasing a copy of this book and sharing this Spanish journey with me (even if you borrowed the book from a friend, or the library and skipped to the end to see how it finished).

Writing this debut novel would not have been possible without the unwavering support of family and friends – in particular my beyond patient and encouraging family who went to practically every flamenco show I ever performed in until they could pretty much replicate all of the choreography. They have been equally supportive of my writing journey.

Massive thanks go to Simone, Ramiro, Natasha and Francesca for their unparalleled Spanish language, cultural and flamenco expertise; to Simone, Steve and Nicole for their dazzling editing insights; to Martine Lleonart for her invaluable structural assessment and belief in my blossoming manuscript; to Graeme Jones from Kirby Jones for his tremendously topnotch typesetting and to the generous and ever-patient Tania for her incredible eagle-eyed editing tips. *Gracias!*

Profoundest thanks to Nadya at Spider House, whose vibrant designs and artistic prowess propelled this book into creative being. I'm so grateful for your generosity, vision and genius!

Huge love to the angels Vicente and Sebastian for sharing your love of Andalucía and flamenco with me; to Manuel Betanzos for your unwavering motivation and passion and to all the treasured flamenco teachers who have taught me over the years – and most especially to Simone for believing in me enough to join her dance troupe in the first place. Thanks to all the cherished adventures shared with my fellow "Funbags" alumni and students (and especially for letting me write about you!). Blessings, too, to the beautiful Jim, whose unique and dazzling light faded far too soon.

Sincerest thanks to Colin – one of our heartfelt conversations inspired the completion of this book and I will forever be grateful for your humility, insight and grace.

To Emilio – my original inspiration for this journey. Your artistry and heartfelt storytelling abilities are a genuine gift to the world. *Muchas gracias.*

And lastly, to Ángel – the most gorgeous soul inside and out. A true kindred spirit who deeply embraces life. You are an absolute *maestro* and an extraordinarily entertaining and generous teacher, performer and human being. Thank you from the depths of my heart for your kindness, brilliance and effervescent joy. I am sincerely honoured to call you a friend. (And equally grateful to Ángel's stunningly talented wife for letting me write such a saucy book about her beloved husband.)

SOBRE LA AUTORA
About the Author

When Stacey – the comedy-loving, boofy-haired-chasing, accidentally-slapstick-yet-highly-sensitive show pony – was first introduced to flamenco, she fell irretrievably into its fiery embrace and enjoyed a decade-long passionate love affair bursting with dynamic rhythms, intoxicating men and even more enchanting accessories.

When she is not being "hangry", looking for a public toilet, or eating carbohydrates – or even when she is – Stacey enjoys sleeping, conversing with cats and watching *Wayne's World* with a side of *Arrested Development*.

Born in a country town at the crack of dawn, Stacey has not been a morning person since.

This debut novel is the result of having too much time on her hands and attempting to relive one of the best months of her life.

¡Olé!

www.wanderswithwit.com

www.ingramcontent.com/pod-product-compliance
Lightning Source LLC
Chambersburg PA
CBHW030252010526
44107CB00053B/1683